Ian Plimer

THE
LITTLE
GREEN
BOOK

For twenties and wrinklies

Published in 2023 by Connor Court Publishing Pty Ltd

Copyright © Ian Plimer

All rights reserved. No part of this book may be reproduced or transmitted in any form or by any means, electronic or mechanical, including photocopying, recording or by any information storage and retrieval system, without prior permission in writing from thepublisher.

Connor Court Publishing Pty Ltd

PO Box 7257

Redland Bay QLD 4165

sales@connorcourt.com

www.connorcourtpublishing.com.au

Phone 0497 900 685

ISBN: 9781922815675

Front Cover: JGD Graphics and Web, Melbourne

Printed in Australia

I find it frustrating, as a lay person, to find answers to technical questions. You see gigantic wind turbines appearing all over the country, but there is very little about the practical value of these monstrosities …
When will common sense and good science prevail and what happens if it does not fairly soon?

Letter from HRH Prince Philip to Professor Plimer, 29th April 2018.

–

This book attempts to answer the questions raised by the late Duke of Edinburgh.

About the author

PROFESSOR IAN PLIMER is Australia's best-known geologist. He is Emeritus Professor of Earth Sciences at the University of Melbourne, where he was Professor and Head of Earth Sciences (1991-2005) after serving at the University of Newcastle (1985-1991) as Professor and Head of Geology. He was Professor of Mining Geology at The University of Adelaide (2006-2012) and in 1991 was also German Research Foundation Professor of Ore Deposits at the Ludwig Maximilians Universität, München (Germany). He was on the staff of the University of New England, the University of New South Wales and Macquarie University. He has published more than 130 scientific papers on geology and was one of the trinity of editors for the five-volume *Encyclopedia of Geology*.

This is his thirteenth book written for the general public, the best known of which are *Telling lies for God* (Random House, 1994), *Milos-Geologic History* (Koan, 1999), *A Short History of Planet Earth* (ABC Books, 2000), *Heaven and Earth* (Connor Court, 2009), *How to get expelled from school* (Connor Court, 2011), *Not for greens* (Connor Court, 2014), *Climate change delusion and the great electricity rip-off* (Connor Court 2017) and *Green Murder* (Connor Court 2021). He frequently publishes newspaper and magazine opinion pieces as well as chapters in books. This book is that of a scientist which has been a labour of love unfunded by third parties.

He won the Leopold von Buch Plakette (German Geological Society), the Clarke Medal (Royal Society of NSW) and the Sir Willis Connolly Medal (Australasian Institute of Mining and Metallurgy). He is a Fellow of the Australian Academy of Technological Sciences and Engineering and an Honorary Fellow of the Geological Society of London. In 1995, he was Australian Humanist of the Year and later was awarded the Centenary Medal. He was Managing Editor of *Mineralium Deposita*, president of the SGA, president of IAGOD, president of the Australian Geoscience Council and sat on the Earth Sciences Committee of the Australian Research Council for many years.

He won the Eureka Prize for the promotion of science, the Eureka Prize for *A Short History of Planet Earth* and the Michael Daley Prize (now a Eureka Prize) for science broadcasting. He was an advisor to governments and corporations and has been a regular broadcaster for decades. He now broadcasts on Sky TV and ADH TV.

Professor Plimer spent much of his life in the the zinc-lead-silver mining town of Broken Hill where an interdisciplinary scientific knowledge intertwined with a healthy dose of scepticism and pragmatism are necessary. Real people live in the bush. He is Patron of Lifeline Broken Hill and the Broken Hill Geocentre. He worked for North Broken Hill Ltd, was a consultant to many major mining companies and has been a director of numerous exploration public companies listed in London, Toronto and Sydney. In his post-university career he is director of a number of unlisted private Hancock Prospecting companies.

A new Broken Hill mineral, plimerite, was named in recognition of his contribution to Broken Hill geology. Ironically, plimerite is green, soft and brittle with an uneven fracture. It is insoluble in alcohol. A ground-hunting rainforest spider *Austrotengella plimeri* from the Tweed Range (NSW) has been named in his honour because of his "provocative contributions to issues of climate change". Maybe *Austrotengella plimeri* is poisonous?

Ian Plimer identifies as $ZnFe_4(PO_4)_3(OH)_5$ and demands the appropriate pronoun be used.

The illustrator uses the pseudonym of AW because of incessant bureaucratic hounding, potential job and income loss by her woke politically-correct government employer and victimisation by those who have chosen not to think critically and logically, use common sense and show respect to others. Her son was a reviewer and gave me helpful comments through the eyes of a child.

A grandson in Canada gave me ideas for Volume 1 and AW gave the idea for the trilogy of books for children. One of the reviewers has to lie low because of her employment in politics. Her comments helped clean up a pretty scrappy first draft and found typos that others missed. This was done under ridiculous time pressures and through the eyes of a non-scientist. Jeff Rayner spent his birthday in a seedy bar in Sarajevo reading the manuscript and made the sort of corrections only a pedant could imagine. As he's on the wagon, these were unassisted by rakija.

My life-long geological friend, John Nethery, was a reviewer of the three volumes, changes were made as a result of his helpful comments. He gave me great encouragement. He is one of those few eminent scientists who has a new discovery named after him, most fittingly in his case a snail. God bless him, and *Georissa johnnetheryi*.

Preface
for twenties and wrinklies

We are all environmentalists. We want a better planet for ourselves and future generations. We do not want to be manipulated, told lies or be bombarded with exaggerated hysteria about the state of the planet. In my life of more than three score and ten years, the planet in my neck of the woods has got better because of greater wealth, technology and environmental awareness.

I have seen a huge improvement in air, water and soil quality; a change from reusing everything because of poverty to recycling; better, more efficient and cheaper consumables and cars; better, more diverse and cheaper food; better health and greater longevity; more disposable cash and the ability to travel cheaply with ease to places we could only dream about when young. The streets are no longer used as effluent drains and places to dump rubbish.

In my lifetime, I have seen the appearance of plumbing systems for water and sewage, extensive public transport, sealed roads and cheap reliable employment-generating electricity. As we became wealthier and wealthier, we used more and more energy and polluted less. As children, we couldn't wait to be an adult in the new modern world and there was no such thing as ecoanxiety.

By now, you may have travelled to a poor country. Look at how many people are not as well off as you. How would you fix this? If you are a true activist you would help others rather than sit around, moan and groan and demonstrate about the state of things. That achieves nothing and will leave you poor all your life.

Do you really believe everything that you are told? Do you believe those trying to part you from your money? Or those trying to gain power or your vote? Or those trying to persuade you to have their political and social views? Did you really learn at school how to look after yourself, survive in the big bad world and to think for yourself?

Very few people at school have been given useful knowledge; were taught to think critically, analytically and independently; were taught how to debate or were taught the difference between verifiable facts and propaganda.

The most useful education you could have received was one where you became literate and numerate and managed to remember a huge amount of material. You would not have been taught about the planet's history. If you can debate and think for yourself, then life will be better.

If you don't have such basic skills, it will be hard to get your interesting dream job on high pay and employment-paid travel to exotic parts of the world. Education is for life and should produce self-sufficient citizens. Will you be one of these? Hard work, thinking for yourself and a sense of morality is all you need to have a great life. I managed, against the odds. You can also.

It is hard for school children to escape from the clutches of incessant negative emotionally-disturbing propaganda that they receive at school regarding the health of the planet. Do you say what everyone else says or can you think for yourself? This brain washing propaganda is disinformation and exploits vulnerability and is easily recognised by jargon, disorganised phrases, repetition, negativity and a lack of logic.

Scientific references to the science in this book are in the references in *Heaven and Earth* and also comprise basic undergraduate geology.

Climate change action is an attempt to change the world into a place with serfs controlled by unelected elites. As I show, it has nothing to do with climate and the environment. If you stand up and argue using facts, you may not end up a serf controlled by an anonymous multinational elite somewhere out there. It's time to deprogram yourself and hit the reset button. Intelligent and knowledgeable people are being silenced such that stupid people won't be offended.

We spend our lives dealing with snake oil salesmen trying to con us and you need to be able to argue, see the fallacy of bland statements and meaningless chants and know how to ask incisive questions such as "*Show me the evidence?*" You need to be trained to spot snake oil at 100 paces.

If you "Google it" or use Wikipedia, then you can be exposed to a body of corrupted biased selective information that is often demonstrably wrong. You are certainly not always gaining knowledge using a search engine. Many computer games are devised by evil people. With some games, you can't proceed until you've killed somebody. Other games teach you to steal and joy ride in luxury cars. This is calculated desensitising of young people to crime.

Here I provide a few uncomfortable and obscure facts, asks questions that you should be asking and expose you to the thread that underpins all science: scepticism.

It is hard to tell people that some teachers are activists with no interest in the nation or children's futures; that many teachers obfuscate and promote disinformation about fundamental science, the environment and history; that they are victims of the left's successful great march through the education system and that a so-called education has not provided children with basic knowledge and the skills to criticise, analyse and argue. It is time to get rid of this nonsense.

The author often is accused of being controversial. If being controversial is to tell the truth, use validated facts and being sceptical of everything, then so be it. We are living in a time of universal deceit and telling the truth is a now a revolutionary act deemed as disinformation.

THE LITTLE GREEN BOOK

For twenties and wrinklies

In the long ago

It was a dark and stormy night on a Thursday 4,567 million years ago when bits of space junk came together to form the Solar System. Ever since that fateful Thursday, climate has been changing for the same reasons it changes today.

In the early days of the Solar System, Jupiter had not yet settled down to hoovering up stray asteroids as it does now and the Earth was constantly bombarded in its first few hundred million years.

Moon made of green cheese

One very large asteroid sliced off a bit of the Earth and this consolidated into our Moon.

There is a theory out there in looney land that the Moon is made of green cheese. This theory can be tested. Some of your Norwegian friends tell you that gjetost cheese has the same seismic wave velocity as lunar rocks. You know that the velocity of seismic waves is related to the composition of the material through which they pass.

Later that night, you check out seismic velocities and find your Norwegian friends were correct. Therefore, our Moon, is made of green cheese and, more specifically, Norwegian gjetost.

Before you nod off that night, you find five reasons why it is impossible for our Moon to be made of green cheese. This is the coherence criterion of science in action. All ideas must be supported by data from other areas of science.

What were the five reasons you worked out to show that the conclusion was incorrect?

Impact craters on the Moon show a history of early bombardment which the Earth also must also have enjoyed. Unlike the Moon, there are no very old craters on Earth because its surface has been constantly reworked but there are smoking guns in the form of asteroid impact debris horizons.

The first atmosphere

The planet was cooling down and leaking gas to form its first atmosphere composed of water vapour, hydrogen, helium, ammonia, methane, carbon monoxide, carbon dioxide and dihydrogen sulphide (rotten egg gas).

Hydrogen and helium escaped into space and, every time the atmosphere cooled enough for water vapour to form rain, the raindrops were boiled off the Earth's hot surface to form water vapour in the atmosphere.

First water and life on Earth

One day, again a Thursday, the Earth's surface was cool enough for pools of water to form on the surface, only to be vapourised by the next asteroid impact. Eventually, when the amount of impacting decreased, pools of water grew to become seas.

The first evidence of running water on the Earth's surface is ancient gravel in western Greenland. You have won the scientific lottery and go on an expedition to the Isua area of western Greenland to look at these gravels.

The old boulders in the gravels are samples of the older source rocks for the gravel. You collect as much ancient gravel as the helicopter can carry. In the laboratory back home you look for fossils.

Nothing. In desperation just before you throw out your precious cargo, you dissolve the rock in extremely aggressive toxic hydrofluoric acid, the one that is released when the lithium batteries in electric vehicles decide to burn. It is also the acid used to etch glass and dissolve rocks.

There is a teaspoon of black residue left. Under the microscope, you see no microfossils. Again, a failure to find the oldest fossils on Earth. Failure is quite normal in scientific research. Before storing the black residue, you check the chemistry of the residue.

Bingo. It has the chemical fingerprint of life and you can feel the first flush of fame forming. You have discovered evidence for the first life on Earth. And you make a perfectly sensible conclusion: As soon as there was water on Earth, there was life.

That life was single-celled bacteria. They can live in hot and cold conditions; in acid and alkaline environments; with or without light; in clouds, snow, salt, soil and rocks; in areas with high radioactivity and in other life and in almost any place you can think of. They are probably still present deep below the Martian surface and could have survived a space trip from Mars to Earth.

The Earth's greatest biomass is not trees or whales. It is bacteria hidden in cracks in rocks in the top 5 km of the Earth's crust. In your body, 90% of cells are bacteria, 15% of your weight is bacterial and you are a creeping colony of critters.

However, your scientific colleagues, many of whom are close personal friends, start to argue with you. Did your samples get contaminated with bacteria during transport and laboratory preparation? Is there earlier life not yet found in older rocks? Did this life spontaneously appear on Earth? How did it happen? Was the Earth seeded by bacterial life from asteroid impacts on Mars that blasted bits of the Martian surface to Earth? Was earlier life on Earth destroyed by impacts?

Your great scientific discovery opened up a hornet's nest of argument. The science was certainly not settled and scientists were doing what they should do: Argue, be sceptical and seek other lines of validated and corroborating evidence. The appearance of life on Earth could only happen once. It was unprecedented.

Heavy rains, big floods, a very hot day and other extreme weather events in your life are not unprecedented. They are within variability, have occurred many times in the past and past extreme weather events are far greater than anything that is measured today. Ignore media hype by those too lazy to find out about the past.

Most extraordinary human deaths on Earth have never been from climate change. They were from volcanic eruptions, earthquakes, tsunamis, war and political stupidity such as communism that killed hundreds of millions of people, mainly by starvation. There are all sorts of cool ways to be wiped out. The really classy ones are asteroid impacts and Carrington events (Look that up. I'm not here to do everything for you).

This early life was simple single-celled bacteria without a

cell nucleus. It was happy to do what bacteria do: Multiply. A few hundred million years later, bacterial colonies and reefs appeared not unlike the modern stromatolites we see in a few parts of the world today. The Earth's atmosphere had evolved into the planet's second atmosphere, a carbon dioxide-rich atmosphere that lasted a few billion years.

First ice age

A few hundred million years later we see bits of material in Africa that were left behind by retreating ice. We don't know much about this early ice age 2,900 million years ago which lasted for about 150 million years because old rocks get bent, smashed up and melted so there is little left to work with.

However, it does tell us that the Earth changed from a warm wet volcanic hothouse planet into an icehouse planet and then back to a warm wet volcanic hothouse planet. Climate changes then were far greater than anything we experience today.

The next ice age

A number of other glaciations, called the Huronian, occurred between 2,400 and 2,100 million years ago. At the same time, the Great Oxidation Event started.

So here you are, the great prize-winning scientist who found evidence for the first life on Earth and you are asked for your expert opinion. Anyone can have an opinion. There is a huge chasm between the opinion of a dogmatic dribbling drongo or activist and an expert.

By now you are famous and have chemists, astrobiologists, microbiologists, astronomers, geologists and mineralogists fawning over you. You propose a theory to explain the Huronian and Great Oxidation Event. Scientific theories change over time with new data so you need to read widely because science is interdisciplinary, evidence comes from a diversity of sources and models are not evidence.

With your theory, you suggest that retreating ice sheets left behind debris comprising boulders, pebbles, Coke bottles, sand, silt, mud, bits of fingernails with pink nail polish and rock flour.

The oceans became fertilised with nutrients from the rock flour, bacteria said "Yippee" to each other, thrived and diversified into a bacterium with a cell wall and a cell nucleus that surrounded and protected all the genetic and metabolic bits.

This new bacterium started to use solar energy, nutrients and water for photosynthesis. There was an explosion of life and traces of oxygen first appeared in the atmosphere.

Genocide

The older bacteria without a cell nucleus were almost totally wiped out during an event of bacterial genocide by a poisonous gas. Bacteria with a cell nucleus emitted oxygen which oxidised and killed the cells with no nucleus. Genocide refugees are still hiding in bogs and swamps, your stomach and at the bottom of some lakes and seas.

This genocide was unprecedented. Your scientific colleagues again argued that this process could have been a once off, could have been stepwise or could have occurred many times until the bacteria perfected the process.

Just because you are a famous expert does not mean that your theory is accepted, even by your friends. Your friends are real scientists and do not accept your scientific authority and fame. They are independent, make conclusions based on evidence and argue against you. They still are your friends, although at times dreadfully annoying.

The Great Oxidation Event

This new oxygen in the air oxidised soils from green to red, it dissolved in the oceans and dissolved iron was oxidised and precipitated on the ocean floor with silica to form layered muds called banded iron formations. There were many later events of oxygenation that produced younger banded iron formations.

These layered muds were hardened and more than two thousand million years later were exposed to the air in tropical conditions. Wait a minute! We had glaciations and then later tropical conditions. Isn't this climate change? And these changes were far greater than those being predicted for your lifetime.

Your colleagues showed you that thick ice sheets in Huronian times were at sea level and at the equator. Over the last 100 million years, oxidised warm tropical acid rain leached out silica from the banded iron formations and the iron content increased from 15% to 60%.

This is how the iron ore that is mined in the Pilbara of Australia, Brazil and West Africa formed. Without iron, used to make steel and reinforced concrete, there would be no modern world. We should have an International Bacteria Day to honour bacteria.

Between 2,400 and 2,100 million years ago bacteria started to give us the oxygen we breathe and the iron we use and this was probably triggered by climate change.

Your theory is concluded with a grand statement (Drum roll please): *"During the Great Oxidation Event, life, water, air and rocks interacted. They still do. Nothing has changed. Unless you change the fundamental laws of physics and chemistry, the processes operating in the past are those that still operate today."*

During the thunderous applause you can only think of more gongs, awards and fame. You join all other scientists with huge egos, personality weaknesses and a dependence on government grants of taxpayer's money to stay alive.

Sometime before or during the Huronian, the continents had become so thick that instead of flipping small land masses to allow the escape of heat, the continents pushed against each other and pulled apart in a process we call plate tectonics.

Continents over the poles became frozen. Continent edges and submarine mountains deflected heat-carrying ocean currents. Some climate cycles appeared due to plate tectonics, others due to changes in the energy emitted by the Sun and the Earth's galactic address.

The second atmosphere

At the time of the Huronian there was up to 20% carbon dioxide in the atmosphere. This was the planet's second atmosphere which lasted for two billion years.

You realise that there have been billions of years and at least four major ice ages when the atmosphere contained tens to hundreds of times more carbon dioxide than now.

Some of these ice ages lasted for tens to hundreds of millions of years. Some carbon dioxide was being removed by photosynthetic bacteria, by bacterial colonies, by soils and by shallow warm water marine precipitates such as the calcium magnesium carbonate called dolomite. Even after this natural sequestration, there was still a hundred times more carbon dioxide in the atmosphere than now.

This does not add up to the story that you have heard from climate activists that trace additions of carbon dioxide added by humans to our current atmosphere of 0.04% carbon dioxide will cause runaway global warming or a climate catastrophe. (*Note to self: Have I made a fundamental mistake? Check the data again. Something is seriously wrong. Rather than trying to get a news headline on some scary scientific claim, I must be sceptical of my own conclusions. Must talk to my chemist friends. I have many because I am now famous. Not famous in my own lunch time but really really famous*).

The Boring Billion

After the Great Oxidation Event, there was the Boring Billion. Although this suggests that nothing much happened for a billion years and 17 milliseconds, it really means that there were no great fundamental changes to life on Earth.

Through the eyes of those exploring for and mining metals, the Boring Billion was when giant mineral deposits formed such as the world's largest lead-zinc-silver deposits (e.g. Broken Hill, Cannington, Mount Isa, McArthur River, Australia;

Gamsberg, Aggeneys, South Africa; Sullivan, Canada) and copper deposits (e.g. Olympic Dam, Mount Isa, Australia).

Without copper and silver, there would be no electronics industry. Without zinc, steel could not be protected from rust. Without lead, internal combustion engines in cars could not start.

During the Boring Billion, the planet was warm and wet with sea level far higher than now. This was the normal state of our planet which has only enjoyed ice sheets for less than 20% of its life. We live in one of those times.

The giant supercontinent of Rodinia started to fragment 830 million years ago, bits of continents collided with other bits, there were massive lava flows on land and on the sea floor and ocean currents changed, as did the climate.

The biggest climate change of all time

You don't have to be Einstein to guess what the planet was like during a period of time known as the Cryogenian which lasted from 720-635 million years ago. It was cold. Extremely cold. Kilometre-thick ice sheets formed at sea level at the equator. This is something we do not see today.

What started the greatest climate change ever? How did the Earth escape from such an intense ice age and change to become warm and wet? Will it happen again? There are great scientific questions that scientists get into an argumentative lather about and there is certainly no consensus, something that does not exist in real science.

The first big event was the Sturtian ice age from 710-660 million years ago. This was the time of snowball Earth when ice sheets covered the land and sea ice covered the water.

During the peak of the Sturtian ice age which waxed and waned many times, there were continents and ocean deeps. There was no continental shelf. Sea level must have dropped at least 600 metres. Bacteria survived in and under ice.

The first complex life

When the ice started to melt and sea level rose, the edge of continents were covered by warm shallow water. Nutrient-rich rock flour dumped by retreating ice was washed into the oceans, nutrients were gobbled up by bacteria after a long cold period and some bacteria evolved into multicellular animals.

These are seen in the 660-million year old Arkaroola Reef in South Australia where some weird coral-like critters occur. There were attempts to form multicellular life before the Sturtian ice age but this life did not survive. This is the first known multicellular life on Earth. This was unprecedented.

Up until a decade or so ago, the oldest known preserved multicellular life on Earth was the 583-542 million year-old soft-bodied Ediacaran fauna. The science was settled. We all knew the Ediacaran was the oldest multicellular life on Earth. That was until more fieldwork was done and the older Arkaroola Reef was discovered. This shows that science is never settled.

Someone somewhere will probably find multicellular life older than the Arkaroola Reef. It is the height of arrogance to think that science is settled. If the science of climate was settled, then there would be no reason to fund any climate science ever again.

The Arkaroola Reef was left high and dry when the Marinoan ice age began. Sea level dropped some 600 metres and thick ice sheets formed at sea level at the equator from 654-632 million years ago. There was no continental shelf. Continental masses were covered by thick ice and deep oceans were covered by sea ice. Bacteria survived under and in the ice and the first attempt at multicellular life died out.

If we had another ice age like the Marinoan, Sturtian or Huronian, all multicellular life would be wiped out and we would have to start the evolutionary clock again. On an evolutionary rerun, you might appear as a hominid with two heads, long ears that you keep tripping over and toenails in your nostrils. Who knows?

Oceans covered by sea ice prevented ocean current circulation of oxygen. Iron oxides in sea floor sediments dissolved in sea water. As soon as the sea ice started to break up at the end of the Marinoan, ocean currents were oxygenated.

The dissolved iron in the sea water precipitated to form sediment-hosted iron ore deposits. Some sea ice had bits of old glaciers that contained trapped boulders which, when the ice started to melt, dropped them on to the sea floor.

Nutrients were washed into the oceans out of glacial debris left by retreating ice. Sea level rose, covered the continental shelf with warm shallow water and bacteria had another go at forming multicellular life. Success.

There was a long period of time when the oceans were warm and nutrient rich and the soft-bodied Ediacaran fauna thrived, diversified and some even had primitive alimentary canals and backbones. These are your not-so-pretty very distant relatives.

Why did the Ediacaran life evolve after the Marinoan and not during the long warm times of the Boring Billion? Was a certain atmospheric oxygen and ocean nutrient level required? Again, these are questions scientists argue about.

In many places, the Marinoan glacial debris is covered by the calcium magnesium seawater precipitate called dolomite. Your chemist friends become curious and try to find out under what conditions dolomite precipitates from sea water.

Their experiments showed that if there is a very high content of carbon dioxide in the atmosphere, dolomite will precipitate as sea water warms.

They use chemical fingerprints in dolomite outcrops to show that precipitation took place at above 30°C whereas the sea ice was at least minus 20°C to cover all the oceans.

A 600-metre sea level rise associated with 50°C warming is serious climate change, not the pathetic few degrees temperature rise predicted for the distant future when the modeller is long dead and bears no responsibility for creating models that don't work.

Ediacaran fauna were bottom scavengers and fed on the algal mats that covered the sea floor at that time. During large storms, algal mats were ripped up from the sea floor, wrapped around Ediacarans and trapped them in a death grip. Ediacaran fossils are a death mask.

The explosion of life

Some Ediacarans got smart and used the dissolved carbon dioxide in seawater to form protective shells. There was an explosion of life 542 million years ago and the soft-bodied Ediacarans were on the menu as were the seafloor algal mats during what was an orgy of predation.

This was the biological big bang in the history of the planet which was unprecedented. All sorts of new critters with a diversity of protective mechanisms formed very rapidly and they were able to swim, burrow, dive, graze, filter feed or take a single big bite for their meal.

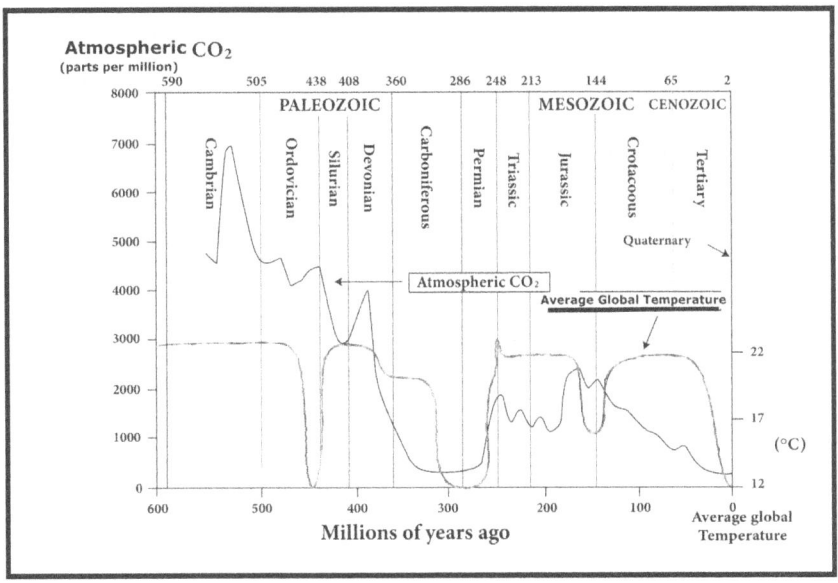

This diagram is all you need to know about climate change. Check out the 542-million year decline in the atmospheric carbon dioxide and the Ordovician, Permo-Carboniferous, Cretaceous and present ice ages. The Earth has been cooling for 50 million years and we have no idea how long the current ice age will last. If atmospheric carbon dioxide drives global warming or climate change, why is there no relationship between atmospheric carbon dioxide and temperature? If carbon dioxide drives climate change, then let's use as much fossil fuel as we can to put carbon dioxide back to where it came from in order to prevent lowering of carbon dioxide to the level where plants starve.

Carbon dioxide from the oceans was used for shells, limestone, reefs, limey muds and black carbon-rich sediments and more and more carbon dioxide was removed from the air via sea water to be sequestered in rocks.

New mountain ranges popped up and rainwater and carbon dioxide from the air formed new soils thereby removing even more carbon dioxide from the air.

We have a much better idea of what the ancient world was like in the last 20% of time because there was less chance of these younger rocks being smashed up, buried deeply and melted.

First plants

Phytoplankton started to thrive in freshwater lakes and again there was an unprecedented event. Fresh water green slime evolved into land plants some 470 million years ago. Amphibians followed soon after to get a feed of land plants.

For the first 90% of the history of the planet there were no land plants, the rates of weathering and erosion were very high and new soils continually got washed into sediment-filled basins. The first land plants thrived and diversified in an atmosphere that contained more than ten times the carbon dioxide content compared to now.

We hear that the Amazonian rainforest is the lungs of the Earth. Wrong. It is the floating phytoplankton in the oceans which have been around for billions of years using carbon dioxide as plant food and excreting oxygen.

It's hard to get emotional about green slime being the lungs of the planet. I have seen many demonstrations with people wanting to save the forests but have never seen a demonstration wanting to protect smelly green slime.

The third atmosphere

The current oxygen-rich atmosphere started to concentrate oxygen some 542 million years ago. It was the planet's third atmosphere. It formed because there was photosynthetic bacteria and an explosion of plant life on Earth. The planet does not de-gas oxygen during cooling. There is no oxygen gas deep in the Earth or other planets.

There is currently 21% oxygen in the atmosphere. At times, the atmospheric oxygen content rose to 35% and there were massive global forest fires far greater than today. With vegetation wiped out by fires, there was an increased rate of soil erosion. At other times during mass extinction events, the oxygen content fell to less than 5%.

Natural sequestration of carbon dioxide

The 542-million-year decrease in atmospheric carbon dioxide began. The atmosphere changed from 0.7% carbon dioxide during the Cambrian explosion of life to the current 0.04%. Land plants, photosynthetic bacteria, marine life and soils are still removing carbon dioxide from the atmosphere. As soon as multicellular life appeared on Earth, atmospheric carbon dioxide started to decrease. It still is.

Death by extinction

Once there was multicellular life, the fossil record of multicellular plants and animals gave a far better record of mass extinctions than the older fossil record of bacteria. There were five major mass extinctions of multicellular life on Earth.

These were 444, 365, 251, 201 and 66 million years ago. A major mass extinction is when 75% of species were wiped out in a short period of time. There have been scores of minor mass extinctions and species turnover is constant with five families wiped out per million years.

Time (million years ago)	Species wiped out	Genera wiped out	Families wiped out
444	86%	57%	27%
365	75%	35%	19%
251	96%	56%	57%
201	80%	47%	23%
66	76%	40%	17%

The extinction of species, genera and families during the five major mass extinctions of multicellular life.

Extinction is a natural part of evolution, cleans out ecosystems, allows new organisms to flourish in the vacated ecology and surviving species better watch out as the new species have more cunning feeding methods. Over time, it was a case of eat or be eaten. It still is.

Over the last 542 million years, there has been increasing species diversity. Extinction is Nature's method of giving evolution a bit of a hurry-up. After Charles Darwin's *Origin of species* was published in 1859, geologists started to construct a geological time scale based on sudden disappearances and appearances of large numbers of new fossil species in rock sequences.

Real scientists argue until they are blue in the face about the causes of mass extinctions and the most popular theories are asteroid impacts, massive volcanicity emitting toxic gas (both underwater and on land), global cooling, biological competition and plate tectonics. There is no evidence from the past that warming leads to extinction.

> **EXTINCTION REBELLION:**
> At its peak, the Extinction Rebellion movement in the UK was paying key activists up to £400 a week to lead anti-fossil fuel demonstrations. Activists were taught to cry on TV, brought young children to demonstrations and manipulated emotions of followers by brainwashing. Don't believe me? Check out what Zion Lights, the former leader of Extinction Rebellion, has to say in Climate Depot (25th January 2023).

> **EXTINCTION REBELLION AND ART:**
> Extinction Rebellion demonstrators threw soup over a famous van Gogh painting in an art gallery and then glued themselves to a wall to demonstrate against the use of oil.

Our species *Homo sapiens* will become extinct, perhaps in the next glaciation. During the process, new species will form and some will snuff it. For example, you may evolve into

many species such as:
- *Homo electronicus,*
- *Homo socialistensis,*
- *Homo dumbeddownschoolingensis,*
- *Homo artificialintelligenis,*
- *Homo fastfoodensis*
- and *Homo veganensis.*

> **CAREFUL WHAT YOU WISH FOR:**
> Extinction Rebellion activists demonstrating against oil glue themselves to roads. The solvent that removes glue is made from oil.

The fossil record shows us that at least four and maybe five of these species will not last long and will become extinct during the next glaciation. I'm not going to do all the work. Tell me which ones will become extinct.

How do we know this will happen to *Homo sapiens*? Because it's happened before. During the last interglacial 128,000 to 116,000 years ago, there were three species of hominids on Earth: *Homo sapiens, Homo floresiensis* and *Homo neanderthalensis* and all with perhaps a common ancestor such as *Homo erectus* and/or *Homo heidelbergensis*.

Some of us carry Neanderthal genes and, although a great story, it's an urban myth that red hair is because of Neanderthal genes.

Early *Homo sapiens* existed 160,000 years ago and perhaps as far back as 300,000 years ago. During the last glaciation from 116,000 to 14,700 years ago, the Toba supervolcano in Indonesia 74,000 years ago polluted the atmosphere so much that tropical vegetation died out and hominids migrated north and south. There were 4,000 surviving breeding pairs. We very nearly became extinct.

Sometime then or a bit later in the last glaciation, *Homo floresiensis* and *Homo neanderthalensis* karked it. My advice is mutate now into another species to avoid the rush and collisions with genetically-engineered flying pigs.

Oh no, not another ice age

An ice age 460-420 million years ago slowed down the diversification of land plants that first appeared 470 million years ago. While plants were becoming established, a large proportion of animal and plant life was wiped out in a major mass extinction 444 million years ago.

The planet bounced back to its normal warm wet volcanic times with a high atmospheric carbon dioxide content. Everything was perfect in this Garden of Eden with no scary reptiles or dinosaurs, just weird forests with no birds and strange fish in the oceans.

It all came to an end with yet another major mass extinction of life 365 million years ago. The planet had been shaken and stirred with huge explosive volcanoes for a while from about 370 million years ago.

The first coal

Plant-decomposing bacteria did not appear until after massive accumulations of land plants between 365 and 251 million years ago. These huge volumes of plant material were compressed into coal. Most of the world's coal formed at this time.

Coal contains 80% carbon which came from atmospheric carbon dioxide resulting in a massive drawdown of atmospheric carbon dioxide. Later, the atmospheric carbon dioxide built up again but not to previous levels. By burning coal, this carbon as carbon dioxide is put back into the atmosphere where it originally came from.

In a forest-rich large underpopulated country like Canada, there are 318 billion trees that use 7.6 billion tonnes of carbon dioxide as food each year. Canadians release 545 million tonnes of carbon dioxide each year from fossil fuel burning, smelting and cement manufacture. Canada is already at Net Zero. Canadians pay tax for the amount of carbon dioxide they release.

In USA, there are 228 billion trees that each year photosynthesise 5.47 billion tonnes of carbon dioxide as plant food. Americans release 5 billion tonnes of carbon dioxide from fossil fuel burning, smelting and cement manufacture each year. The US is already at Net Zero.

In Australia, the grasslands, rangelands, forests, crops and continental shelf waters each year photosynthesise ten times as much carbon dioxide than is released by Australian industry and individuals. Australia is already at Net Zero. Australians pay tax for the carbon dioxide they emit for plants to use as food.

On planet Earth, there are 3 trillion trees that suck up 72 billion tonnes of carbon dioxide as plant food each year. Humans emit 37 billion tonnes of carbon dioxide each year. The planet is already at Net Zero, despite massive emissions from China. Why even bother about Net Zero. Unless, of course, you can make money from it.

And here is the problem. If Canada, the US, Australia and the whole world is at Net Zero, where does the extra modern carbon dioxide come from? It's from degassing of carbon dioxide dissolved in the oceans.

Some 97% of annual emissions are from ocean degassing with minor amounts from volcanoes and animals. Carbon dioxide has an inverse solubility in water. The lower the temperature of water, the more carbon dioxide can dissolve.

Analysis of the chemical fingerprints in ice cores drilled in Greenland and Antarctica show that whenever there has been a natural warming event, the atmospheric carbon dioxide content rises hundreds to thousands of years later. If the oceans warm, they release carbon dioxide. Carbon dioxide does not drive global warming. It's the exact opposite.

After the major mass extinction 365 million years ago, the planet bounced back. It always does except that life afterwards is a bit different. During the Carboniferous and Permian coal-forming times, coals formed in high latitude areas. Other rocks formed in deep ocean settings and settings similar to the modern Persian Gulf with shallow water black marine muds, salt pans and red dune sands.

The Carboniferous Northern Hemisphere coals have a high ash and sulphur content, mainly due to sea level rise and the covering of coal swamps with sulphur-bearing seawater which soaked and stayed in the decomposing plant material. Burning such coals produces sulphur dioxide which ends up as smog and acid rain.

China and Russia still have terrible smogs and acid rain but the rest of the Northern Hemisphere has cleaned up its act. Why? Because they are not totalitarian, are wealthy, could afford to clean up and had a political system whereby community action and health problems were the trigger for environmental action. Look up The Great Smog of London which happened during your grandparent's lives.

Northern Hemisphere Carboniferous coals are not as good quality as the Permian coals from Australia, South Africa, India and Argentina which are low ash and low sulphur. Sulphur pollution is minimal in the Southern Hemisphere and more energy is produced per kilogram of Southern Hemisphere coal than from a kilogram of Northern Hemisphere coal. There are huge unmined coal deposits in Antarctica.

The supercontinent Gondwana

As part of continents moving around and causing supervolcanoes, one supercontinent called Gondwana remained glued over the South Pole for the last 300 million years. If you want to blame something for climate change, then blame the last fragment of Gondwana for having the same address for 300 million years and not moving away from the pole.

In the Permian period between 299 and 251 million years ago, the ancient supercontinent of Gondwana comprised the present-day South Africa, India, Australia, South America and Antarctica. There was an ice age and massive ice sheets advanced and retreated over Gondwana.

During interglacials, monstrous amounts of plant material accumulated in wet high latitude swamps to give thick layers of high-quality Southern Hemisphere peat which later was compressed to coal.

Biggest mass extinction of all time

Around 251 million years ago there was the biggest mass extinction of all time. About 96% of all species were wiped out. The evolutionary clock almost had to start again.

Nearly all plants were wiped out, less than 5% of marine species survived and about a third of all land animals made it, especially those that had burrows.

Do a thought experiment. If 100% of all multicellular species were wiped out 251 million years ago, what would the planet look like now?

There is no scientific consensus about the greatest mass extinction planet Earth enjoyed. The science is certainly not settled. The most attractive idea floating around is that a dirty big asteroid hit Siberia triggering basalt volcanoes, lava covered much of Siberia and filled in the impact crater. Gases such as sulphur dioxide and dihydrogen sulphide (rotten egg gas) belched out of the volcanoes and poisoned the oceans and atmosphere.

Mercury is released during volcanic eruptions and, at that time, mercury was spread wide and far. It is highly toxic and if an animal was struggling to breathe, being hit with an unhealthy dose of poisonous mercury might have pushed it over the edge.

The oxygen content of the oceans dropped and the oceans had a short-lived surface acid layer. Plants and animals were poisoned, especially shallow marine and floating marine critters, and the sulphurous poisonous atmosphere would have reflected light and heat.

After removal of carbon dioxide for coal formation, the atmosphere was replenished with carbon dioxide from planetary degassing by volcanicity. Big scientific questions remain. Why did some plants and animals die and others not? If the carbon dioxide to replenish the atmosphere did not come from volcanicity, where did it come from?

Oh no, not another mass extinction

It took about 10 million years for all ecologies to be filled again after the biggest mass extinction of all time. The planet was back to its normal warm wet volcanic state with high sea levels. And there it stayed until the next inevitable mass extinction of life 201 million years ago. Again, scientists argue about what caused the sudden disappearance of 80% of species 201 million years ago.

The science is certainly not settled. One camp has found a large number of asteroid craters that formed around 200 million years ago and point the finger at a swarm of asteroids that peppered the Earth.

Another camp suggests that there were monstrous submarine supervolcanoes that added poisonous gases to the atmosphere, changed ocean currents and replenished the atmosphere with carbon dioxide. Again, the top of the oceans would have been acid for a short time and highly toxic mercury would have been spread wide and far.

Impacting might have triggered supervolcanoes which would keep both camps happy.

Gondwana breakup

Around 180 million years ago, the Indian Ocean started to form by the pulling apart of continents. Huge flows of basalt formed across southern Africa and on the floor of the Indian Ocean. The planet was again farting out massive quantities of carbon dioxide but no large quantities of sulphur gases and mercury so life was spared from yet another mass extinction.

Birds evolved from dinosaurs about 165-150 million years ago and the primitive call of cockatoos might be the dinosaur in them having a natter.

A couple more ice ages

It was wonderful in the warm wet Jurassic world and then, about 170 million years ago, there was a short sharp ice age. The planet warmed very quickly and then there was another longer ice age 115 to possibly 95 million years ago.

Ice sheets were in polar mountainous areas, glaciers carried material from valley floors to the sea and icebergs melted and dropped boulders onto the sea floor.

Australia was then in a temperate climate near the South Pole. Dinosaurs had large eyes to be able to see in the long dark winters. In the Great Artesian Basin of Australia glacial drop boulders are common and, as a result of later intense tropical weathering along the edge of the Basin, boulders often were coated by opal and fossils were replaced by opal.

Crystals of salts had accumulated underneath icebergs, dropped onto the sea floor and then were later opalised to form "opal pineapples". If you happen to have a few "opal pineapples" floating around, you'll never need to work again

Unprecedented hot times

After this ice age, the planet warmed up again. Some of the hottest times ever experienced on the planet were 92 million years ago. If some activist tries to tell you that today, this month or Wimbledon this year is the hottest since records have been kept, the geological record shows that this is just plain wrong. It's just disinformation aimed at scaring you.

The Cretaceous had hothouse and icehouse conditions, massive volcanic activity and great changes in the atmospheric carbon dioxide content.

Death spiral for plants

Over the last 140 million years, the atmospheric carbon dioxide content has been steadily decreasing. If it halves, then plants will die. With no plants, there will be no animals.

Typical coals contain more than 80% carbon and the rock limestone contains 44% carbon dioxide. Both coal and limestone obtained their carbon originally from the atmosphere.

If we really want to interfere with natural processes, then we should be burning as much fossil fuel as possible and sintering limestone to cement to add the plant food carbon dioxide to the atmosphere.

It might be well and good to go carbon neutral or Net Zero but the plants will not thank you as you help them on their path to oblivion. We are probably only a glaciation or two away from halving the carbon dioxide content of the atmosphere.

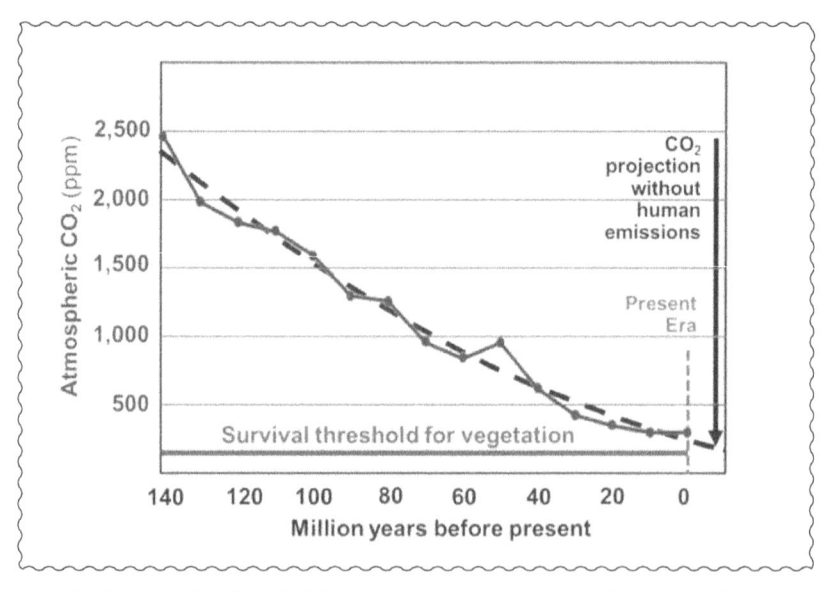

The Berner-Kothavala 2001 long-term decrease in the atmospheric carbon dioxide content showing that, if the trend continues, then plants will have no food. Many people, such as the founder of Greenpeace Dr Patrick Moore suggest that, to save plant life on the planet, you have an environmental responsibility to put carbon dioxide back to where it came from: The atmosphere.

Bye bye Gondwana

Gondwana started to fragment about 130 million years ago. The shape of continents and the ocean floors changed. As a result, heat-carrying ocean currents changed and this affected climate.

By 100 million years ago, Africa had moved northwards and released Madagascar to be on its own, India had moved northwards to eventually collide with Asia and Australia drifted north at about 10 cm a year. It is currently moving northwards at about 7 cm a year.

Then, a great geological event occurred. Australia got rid of New Zealand about 80 million years ago to give them their well-deserved earthquakes and volcanoes. Australia is still pushing New Zealand out into the Pacific, and a good thing too.

Dead dinosaurs

The planet was warm, wet and with high sea levels when there was a mass extinction of life 66 million years ago. This was the end of the dinosaurs and 76% of all species on Earth. There are two scientific stories to explain the mass extinction we all know about.

The favoured theory is that a giant asteroid hit Mexico. Bits of fragmented and vapourised Mexico were blasted into the stratosphere to form a poisonous sulphurous and dust blanket. The planet became dark and plants died from lack of sunlight and poisonous sulphurous acid rain. Animals died and there was a snowball effect of death.

There is something romantic about a dirty big asteroid heading for Earth with "Dead dinosaur" written on it but this may not have been what happened 66 million years ago.

The other theory is that volcanoes on the Deccan Plateau of India belched out huge amounts of lava, poisonous sulphurous gases and carbon dioxide.

The planet recovered, dinosaurs did not, mammals survived and diversified to become a dominant group in the new ecologies that had been vacated.

Mountain building

While all this excitement was going on, continental collision started to push up the Rockies and Andes about 80 to 50 million years ago as the Pacific Ocean pulled apart. The Rockies and Andes are still rising, as shown by the regular volcanoes and earthquakes.

India collided with Asia about 50 million years ago, pushed up the Tibetan Plateau. Because the crust is so thick, there are no volcanoes at this plate boundary but the earthquakes are intense.

The jet stream was interrupted by new mountain chains, rocks chemically reacted with rain and air to form soil and this soil extracted carbon dioxide from the air.

Soil was later removed to form sediment-filled basins flanking mountain ranges. The whole process of soil formation in mountains and sediment removal to basins continues to the present day.

This plate tectonic process has driven past climates and it still does. Why is plate tectonics ignored in climate models or any story whipped up by climate activists?

The planet has been cooling for 4,567 million years. At present, some 70% of the Earth's surface is covered by the oceans. There are millions of known submarine volcanoes on the ocean floor that have released heat and carbon dioxide into the oceans yet these well-documented processes are ignored in climate models. No wonder the models fail.

Hot as Hell, long cooling

Again, the planet experienced very hot times 56 million years ago, far hotter than anything experienced since then. After hot times, what would you expect? Hotter times or cooling?

The planet has been cooling for the last 50 million years and we are again enjoying icehouse conditions with alternating glaciations and interglaciations.

Some climate activists claim that this cooling is due to sucking up of atmospheric carbon dioxide by new soil formation on a new mountain range, the Tibetan Plateau.

However, many mountain ranges formed on Earth well before the Tibetan Plateau and there is no relationship between the formation of massive mountain ranges in the past and the atmospheric carbon dioxide. This theory has been tested and is rejected. That's how science works.

There is no relationship between carbon dioxide and global temperature over time. In periods of high atmospheric carbon dioxide, there were ice ages. According to the climate activist story, this should not happen. In periods of low carbon dioxide, we had hothouse times. Please explain?

One lonely gas molecule

Climate activists claim that a few parts per million increase in atmospheric carbon dioxide resulting from human activities will lead to unstoppable global warming, a climate crisis or a climate catastrophe.

Any real scientist would immediately say *"Show me"*. The atmospheric carbon dioxide is about 420 ppm which is one molecule of carbon dioxide in 2,500 other molecules in air. If humans emit 3% of the annual emissions of carbon dioxide, then only one molecule of carbon dioxide in 83,333 molecules in air is of human origin.

Other major planetary and solar processes such as the Earth's orbit, the Sun's emissions of energy and plate tectonics have the grunt to change another planetary process such as climate.

Do you really think that this one lonely molecule of plant food in 83,333 other molecules in the thin atmosphere can change a major planetary process such as climate?

If you do, you'd better mount your unicorn and ride to the bottom of the garden to speak to the fairies to get reassurance.

Extraordinary ideas need extraordinary evidence, especially in the light of the fact that it has never been shown that human emissions of carbon dioxide drive global warming and that, in the past, natural global warming has been followed by an increase in atmospheric carbon dioxide thousands of years later.

Climate activists claim this lonely single carbon dioxide molecule is responsible for modelled future catastrophic man-made global warming, now rebadged as climate change.

They then predict that a few extra carbon dioxide molecules of human origin will lead to unstoppable global warming and a climate crisis. Pull the other one, it's got bells on it. The past shows a very different story to what we are being told.

Either climate "science" speculative models are wrong or all geology is wrong. If all geology is wrong, then why do we continue to find hidden mineral and energy resources at depth using geological measurements? Climate models are a naïve attempt to try to predict the future and are not data. They don't even use existing data.

Failed models

Over 100 climate model predictions of future temperature compared with temperature measurements from balloons and satellites show that the scary models of a fry-and-die future are wrong.

Not just wrong but hopelessly wrong. Models are based on the assumption that carbon dioxide drives climate change. If the models are wrong, then the assumption is also wrong. It is.

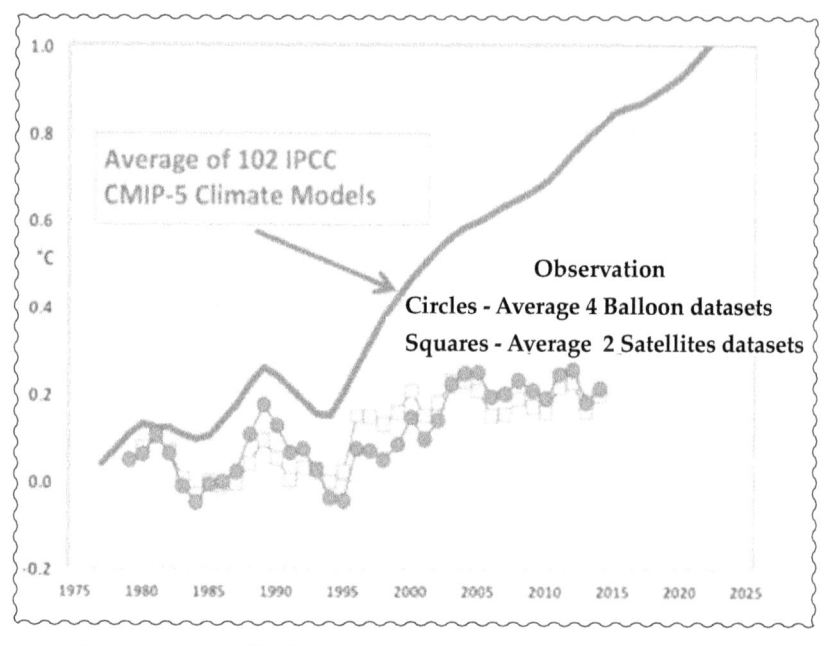

The average of 102 IPCC climate models that attempted to predict future temperature compared to Christy's measurements from 4 balloon and 2 satellite data sets. Even over a 40-year period, the predictions were wrong and clearly predictions for temperature over the next 100 or 200 years will also be wrong. Climate is not understood and the past is ignored. When such models are run backwards, they cannot show what has happened in the past.

If it cannot be measured, then it does not exist. When faced with a choice of measurements or models, measurements win because they are repeatable validated data whereas models are not data but speculations about the future. Good for a laugh but not worth getting into a sweat about. Or changing the country's energy systems.

End of rant. Back to Earth history.

The modern ice age

Plate tectonics led to the separation of South America from Antarctica. The Drake Passage opened 34 million years ago. A circum-polar current isolated Antarctica from warm tropical waters coming from the north. This last bit of Gondwana developed an ice sheet in our current icehouse times. There were relatively warmer times, such as 20 million years ago, but the Earth was still in an icehouse.

The Greenland ice sheet has existed continuously for the last 18 million years and has been influenced by warm waters entering the Arctic via the Bering Strait between Russia and Alaska and from the North Atlantic Ocean. It may have had some ice off-and-on in the period between 56 and 34 million years ago.

Humans

Both the great apes and primitive humans have the same ancestor some 6 or 8 million years ago. The ability for humans to walk on two legs evolved about 4 million years ago.

About 20 different species of early humans have been recognised. Humans started to migrate out of Africa about 1.8 to 2 million years ago and dropped in on Europe about 1.5 to 1 million years ago. They kept spreading and migrating. Humans still do.

During our current ice age, we were distant from the Sun (glaciation) or closer to the Sun (interglacial) in a 100,000-year orbital cycle. Humans struggled during cycles of 90,000 years of glaciation. During the last glaciation humans almost became extinct when the atmosphere was filled with dust from the Toba supervolcano 74,000 years ago. One of the coldest times in the history of the planet became even colder.

Humans have the enzyme protease to metabolise meat and teeth to rip meat off bones. They had a mixed diet as herbivores and opportunistic carnivores. In times of plenty, fruit sugars kept the brain functioning. In hard times, the brain survived on fat.

This remarkable evolutionary human characteristic allowed humans to survive glaciation. If ever you get obese, eat like humans did during times of glaciation.

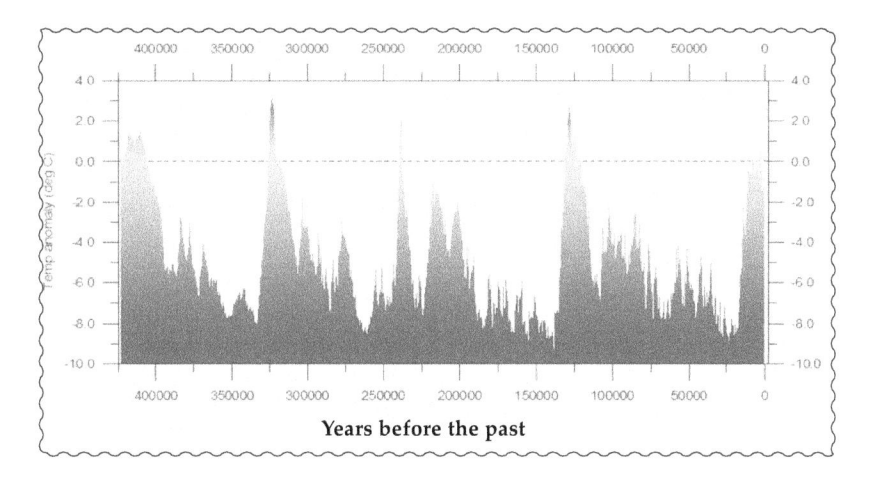

Temperatures from ice cores showing cycles of 90,000 year-long glaciations and 10,000-year-long interglacials. Our current interglacial is not as warm or as long as previous interglacials. There were rapid warmings of up to 10°C and very rapid short sharp temperature changes during glaciation. Although tools and weapons improved technically during this time, one of the greatest inventions was the bone needle which allowed animal skins to be sown into warm clothing for the extremes of cold.

Climate: The day before yesterday

Climate is about patterns over hundreds and thousands of years and not a single hot day, week, year or decade. Over 100,000-year cycles, the planet's temperature dropped and then warmed without the help of a single carbon dioxide-emitting coal-fired power plant.

During glaciation, there were short sharp periods of cooling and warming. The rates of warming were far higher than anything measured today and clearly had nothing to do with burning fossil fuels. In our current interglacial, the best-known cold period during the post-glacial warming was called the Younger Dryas from 12,900-11,600 years ago.

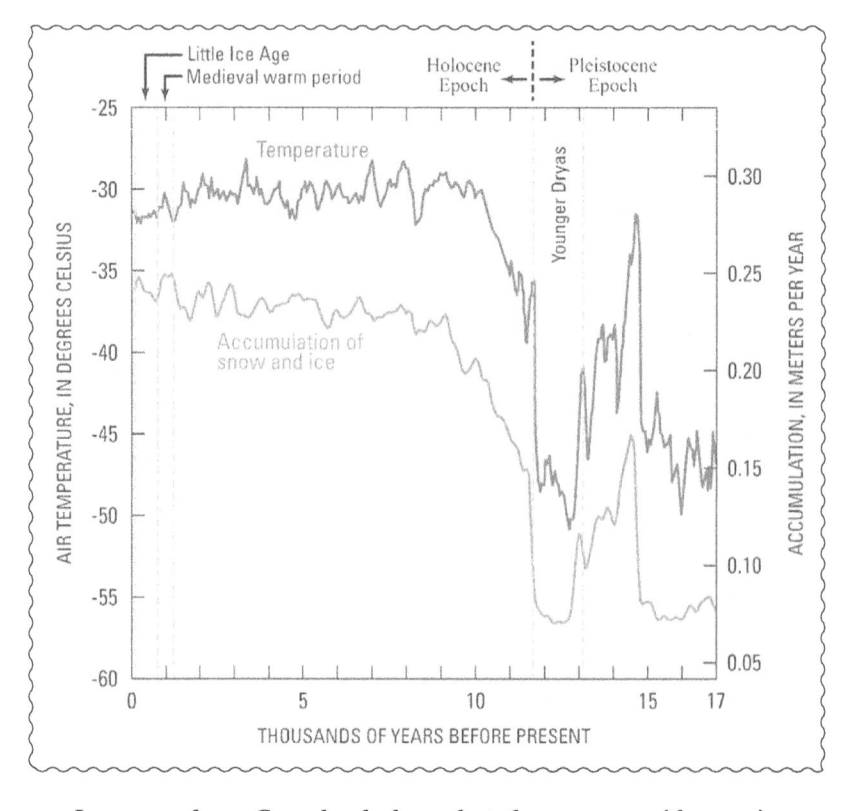

Ice cores from Greenland show that there was rapid warming after the Younger Dryas of at least 15°C. Humans did not die from this global warming. It was the exact opposite. They thrived. The rate of temperature increase was far greater than even the most unbalanced catastrophist suggests for the current warming event.

It resulted from armadas of icebergs in the Atlantic Ocean from ice sheet collapse in Canada and Greenland. The oceans and air cooled. Humans started to live in fortified villages, grow grain rather than collect grain seeds in the bush and they domesticated quieter non-carnivorous animals like cattle and sheep.

At last, the cool and warm interglacial

The present interglacial started 14,700 years ago and may have finished 4,000 years ago as we plunge into the next orbitally-driven cold period. During this cooling trend, there have been periods when it was warmer than now such as in Minoan, Roman and Medieval times and colder during the Dark Ages and Little Ice Age. There was no fossil fuel burning in Minoan, Roman and Medieval times yet it was warmer than today.

Great empires developed in warm times when there was excess food and wealth, people lived longer, and there was less disease and war. Excess wealth was used in Roman times to build roads, bridges and buildings, many of which still exist today. In cold times, there was crop failure, starvation, disease, more wars and people died young.

If you are told the planet is warming, your reply must be "*Since when?*" The planet has been cooling since Minoan times. It also cooled since Roman times. It has warmed since the Dark Ages, cooled since the Medieval times and warmed since the Little Ice Age from 1200-1850 AD. It is deceptive to blandly state that the planet is warming.

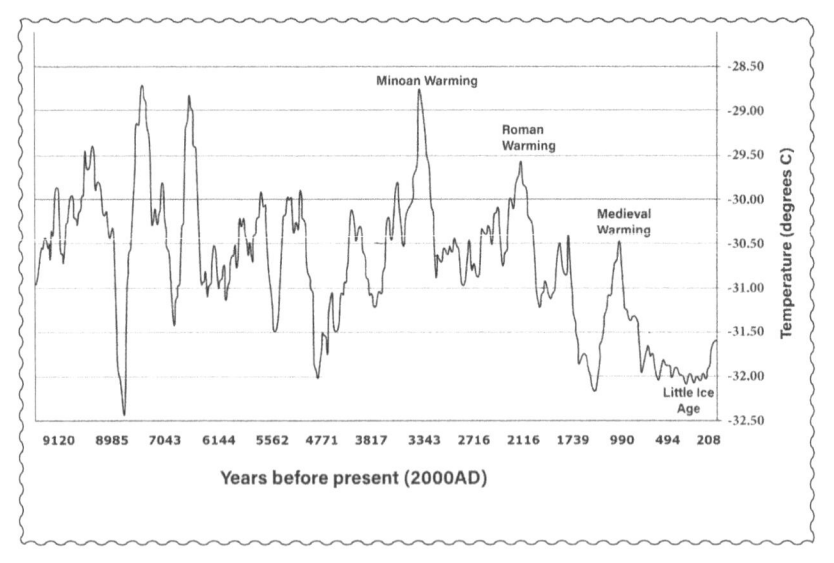

Proxy measurements in Greenland ice core showing the last 10,000 years of our current interglacial. The peak of the interglacial was probably from 7,000-4,000 years ago. Since then, there has been a 4,000-year period of cooling with spikes of warming and cooling.

The Minoan Empire was wiped out by the explosive Santorini volcanic eruption at about 1600 BC. The Dark Ages saw off the Romans. From 535-545 AD, the lack of sunspots showed that the energy from the Sun had decreased. Massive volcanic eruptions at that time in Papua New Guinea, central America and Iceland filled the atmosphere with dust and poisonous sulphur gases.

People coughed themselves to death, the weakened population was killed off by the plague, crops failed, starvation killed people and it was dark, wet and cold. Don't give me the good old days. They weren't.

A more energetic Sun led to the end of the Dark Ages and there was 400-year period of wonderful warm weather during the Medieval Warming. It was warmer than now and sometimes there were two grain harvests each summer. Excess wealth in Europe was used to build the great cathedrals, universities and monasteries.

No fossil fuels were burned then to make the planet warm. These were natural climate variations, far greater than anything predicted now by even the most hardened catastrophist.

Eric the Red was appealing to people to populate Greenland where there were cattle and sheep. Barley and oats were grown and graves could be dug because there was no permafrost. None of that could happen today in Greenland.

It only took 23 years to change from the Medieval Warming to the Little Ice Age. Ice appeared in the Gulf of Bothnia between Finland and Sweden in 1303 AD and it was all downhill after that. Each time there was a period of reduced or no sunspots, it became even colder. Rivers and canals froze, there were ice fairs on the rivers and oxen were cooked on spits on the river ice.

During cold times in the Little Ice Age, crops failed, there was starvation and disease. Natural cycles of climate were not understood and, of course, someone had to be blamed.

Many women were killed during the coldest times of the

Little Ice Age because it was thought that they were witches causing crop failures. This is a good example of emotion with no evidence. The emotional hysteria of human-induced climate change today is little different.

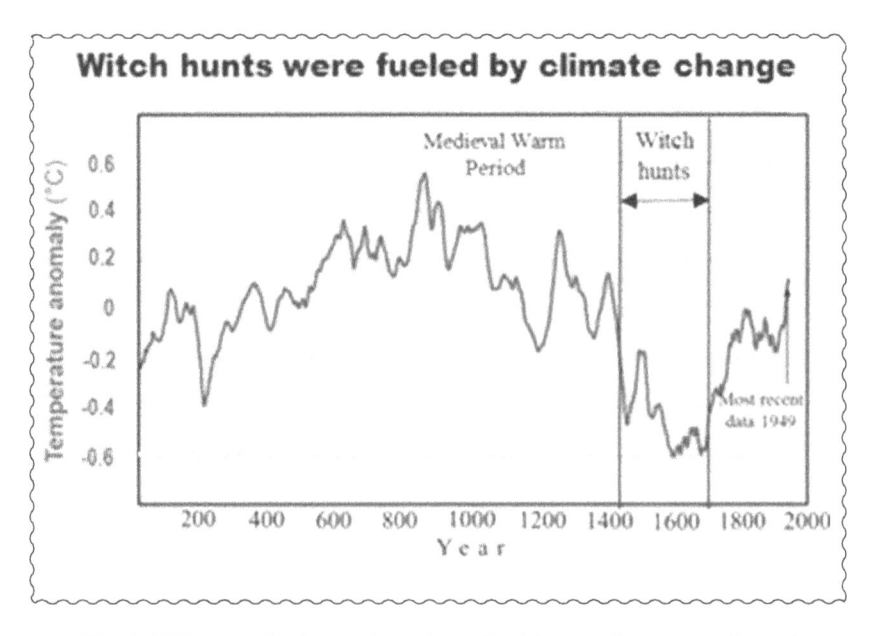

Witch hunts were fueled by climate change

Witch killing took place when there had been a large number of extremely cold months.

After the killing of witches in the coldest period of the Little Ice Age, the Maunder Minimum, the planet started to warm up. Did killing witches warm the planet or did the Sun start to release a little more energy? Solar fingerprints such as carbon 14 in sediments show that the Sun became a little more active and released more energy.

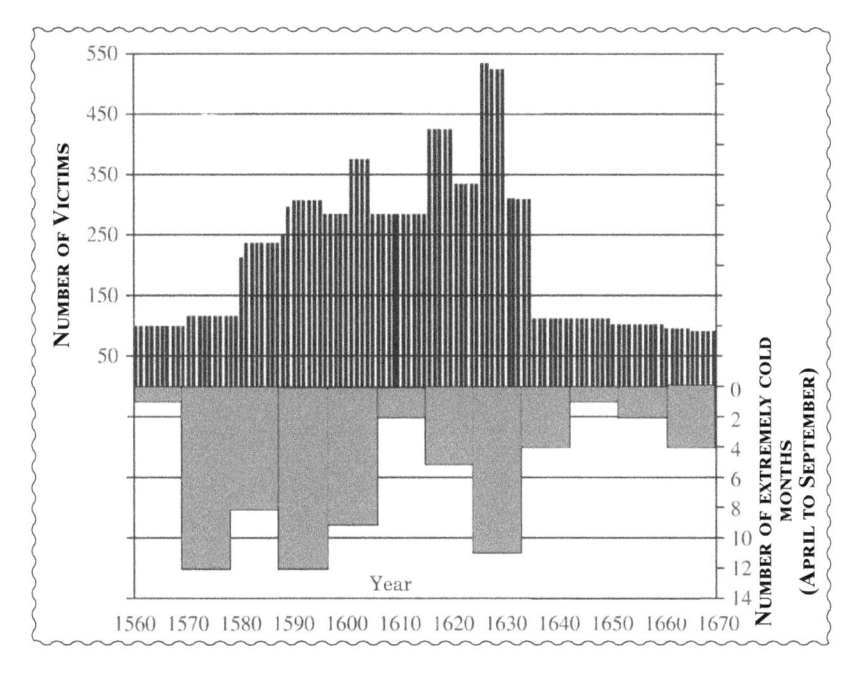

During the coldest period of the Little Ice Age, witch killing took place. After witches were killed, the climate started to warm.

If the Sun's magnetic field contracts with changes in solar activity, more carbon 14 and other isotopes form in the atmosphere. This will also occur if an atomic bomb is exploded or there is a distant supernova explosion.

Changes in solar energy emissions can be measured and computed as the total solar intensity. Reconstructions of the past solar activity can be made by measurement of new isotopes generated in the atmosphere. These drop to Earth with rain and dust particles.

The Sun has now entered a Grand Solar Minimum which solar physicists think will last from 2020-2053 AD. If you are a witch, head for the hills. You can never be too sure.

With abundant energy and better buildings, we are far better equipped for cool and warm events compared to previous generations.

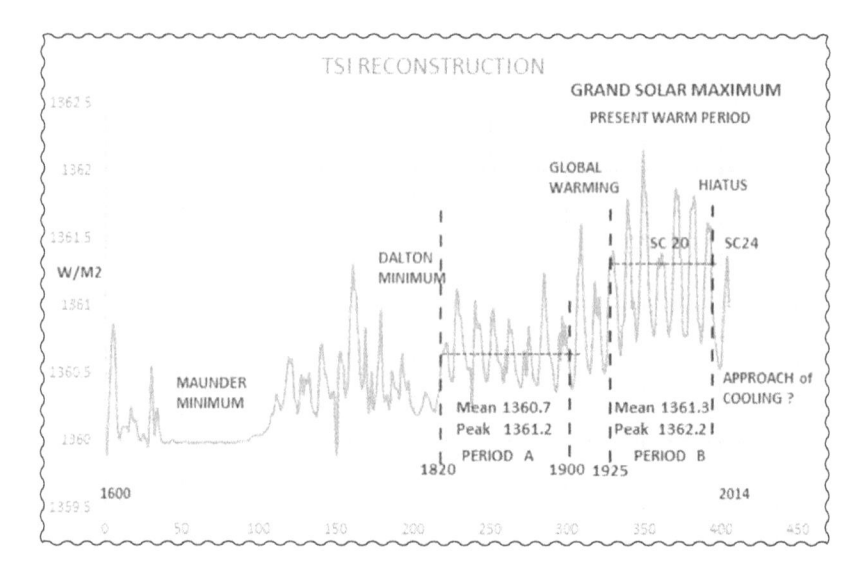

The reconstruction of the total solar irradiance from the Maunder Minimum to the present using Solar Cycles. It was during the Dalton Minimum that Napoleon entered Moscow on 14th September 1812. Moscow was abandoned and had been set alight. Of the 600,000 soldiers who left France, only 100,000 returned home on foot from Russia in a bitter Dalton Minimum winter. The current Grand Solar Minimum has just started. If you want to invade Russia, do it now before the middle of the next cool minimum.

Many scientists don't think that human emissions of carbon dioxide are warming the planet. These people get cancelled or go to Facebook gaol but fortunately don't suffer the same deathly fate as witches. In today's world, many of these people lose their jobs for thinking differently. We've seen it all before.

Whoops, a mistake or two

Climate change policy is one of the most costly and undemocratic policy mistakes for generations and you will pay dearly. A previous one was communism.

Climate change activism is the greatest scientific fraud for generations. A previous one was Lysenkoism in communist Soviet Union which led to the death by starvation of at least 30 million people. Scientists were imprisoned and killed for disagreeing with Lysenko's rejection of genetics.

Scientists tend to reach consensus when you censor, sack, fail to employ, imprison or kill those who don't.

It is claimed that there has been human-induced warming since the Industrial Revolution in the early 1800s. Of course. The early 1800s was in the Little Ice Age.

Would you expect it to cool or warm after the Little Ice Age?

Industrial revolution and climate

What has been measured since 1850 are three very slight warmings and two slight coolings. The rate of warming was the same for all three warmings yet the carbon dioxide emissions increased greatly. If carbon dioxide drives global warming, then the rate of warming should have increased. It didn't.

The other evidence that human carbon dioxide emissions do not drive warming are the two cooling trends. If human emissions of carbon dioxide drive warming, then why was there cooling?

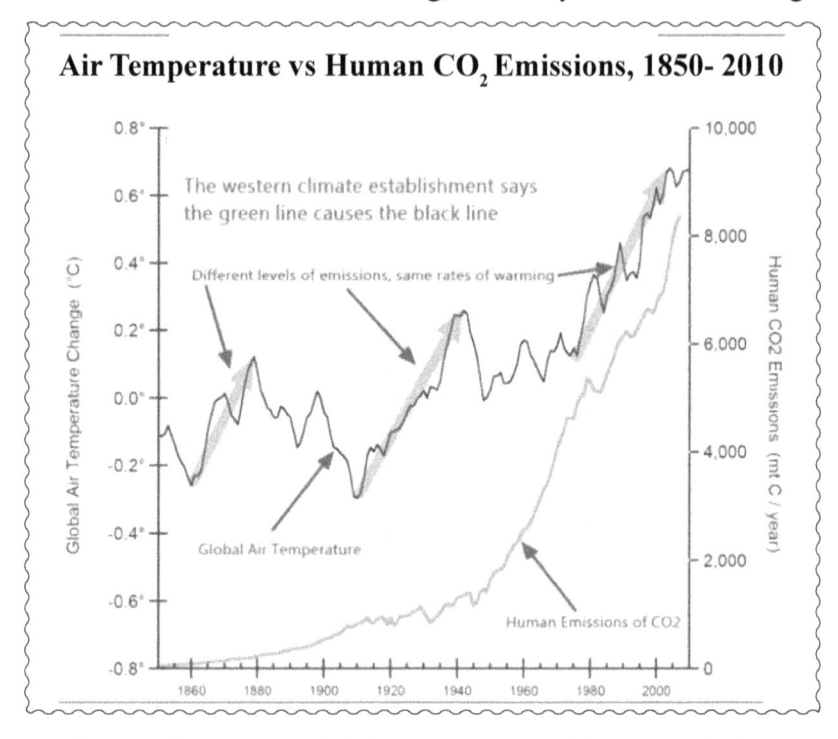

Air Temperature vs Human CO_2 Emissions, 1850- 2010

The western climate establishment says the green line causes the black line

Different levels of emissions, same rates of warming

Global Air Temperature

Human Emissions of CO2

Changes in average global temperature and human emissions of carbon dioxide since 1850 showing no relationship between temperature and human emissions of carbon dioxide.

If all previous warmings were natural, then you'd better provide some pretty convincing repeatable evidence in accord with all other data that the warming since the 1850s is human-induced and not part of the natural cycles of cooling and warming. I've been waiting for decades.

In your lifetime, the atmospheric carbon dioxide content has been increasing and the temperature static or decreasing. Why bother about climate change and carbon dioxide emissions when no relationship exists? Why bother when the biggest emitters do nothing and don't care?

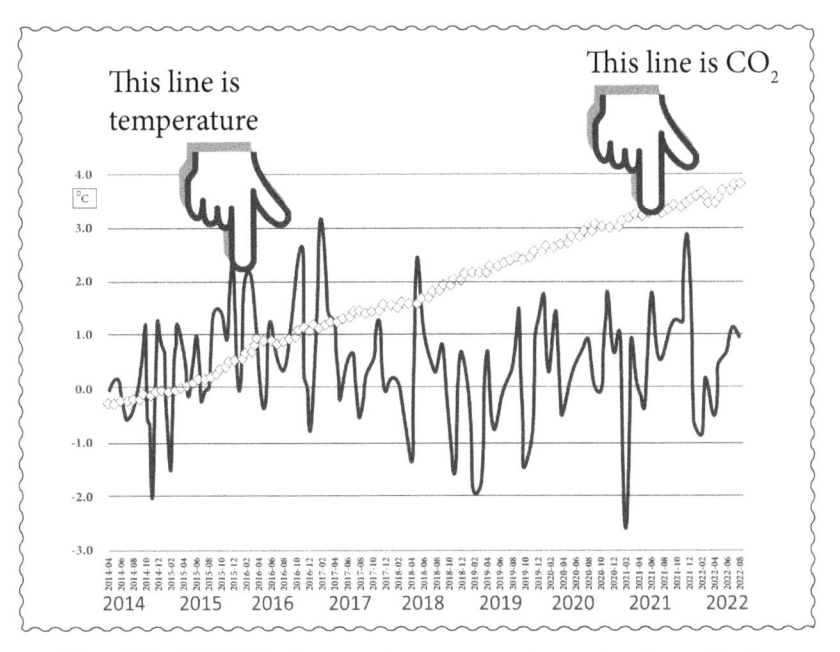

The US USCRN temperature anomaly and atmospheric carbon dioxide trends between August 2015 and August 2022. Measurements show no relationship between temperature and carbon dioxide.

It is the past proxy data and measurements that kill off the hysteria about human-induced global warming. No wonder climate "scientists" will not debate me or other geologists. It is only data that could show I'm wrong, not abuse, cancellation or feelings.

No wonder the Intergovernmental Panel on Climate Change (IPCC) does not have geologists on the panel. The IPCC is a political organisation specifically established to show that only human emissions drive global warming. Every now and then they release a hysterical summary report for politicians and the media which is unrelated to their lengthy scientific reports that ignore the past.

The past is the key to the present and is written in stone. Human-induced climate change could only be validated by reproducible evidence in accord with other evidence. The theory of human-induced climate change is not in accord with the evidence from the past and, like so many scientific theories over time, must be rejected.

For example, we know of the very cold periods in the Little Ice Age from a knowledge of history, cosmogenic isotopes, solar physics, geology, micropalaeontology, ice core drilling, literature and even landscape paintings which showed cloudiness at certain periods of time.

We can be very confident that all past cold and warm periods were natural. The claim that only the latest warm period is of human origin and the others were not ignores all we know of the past. This is not science. It is propaganda.

Climate cycles

We also know natural cycles of climate are driven by many factors and that the IPCC ignores tectonic and galactic factors and greatly downplays the role of that great ball of heat in the sky, the Sun.

Constant Cyclical Climate Change
KNOWN CYCLES

400 million years	tectonic
143 million years	galactic
100,000 years	orbital
41,000 years	orbital
23,000 years	orbital
1,500 years	solar
210 years	solar
87 years	solar
60 years	ocean
18.7 years	lunar
11 years	solar

Every 400 million years or so, continents break up, drift about and even cross poles. A bad galactic address every 143 million years is when Earth is bombarded with more cosmic radiation, clouds form and the planet cools. The Milankovitch cycles of orbit bring the Earth closer or more distant from the Sun which also emits variable amounts of energy. The ancient Chinese calendar was based on 60-year crop cycles driven by a change in ocean currents. Every 60 years when warm water was pushed towards the North Pole, the Northwest Passage was navigable. Every 18.7 years, lunar tidal forces push warm water towards the North Pole and there is a sudden reduction in sea ice. The Earth's magnetic field has flipped 183 times over the last 83 million years yet this does not appear to have changed climate. This table shows that it is not possible to deduce climate changes from observation of one hot day, week, year, decade or century. The only way to understand climate is to view climate change cycles over deep time.

We see these climate cycles preserved in all sorts of modern and ancient sediments and fossils from the ocean deeps, continental shelf, reefs, lakes, swamps and bogs. Sea level changes over the last 542 million years (Vail Curves) have been calculated and used successfully in oil exploration.

They are far more detailed than those calculated by academic scientists. Vail Curves are also cyclical, show that sea level fell some 130 metres during the latest glaciation and, at times when there was no ice, sea level was 200 metres higher than at present. Even greater sea level changes are recorded from the Cryogenian.

In our current interglacial, we see cycles of warming and cooling on a different scale from some of the earlier geological diagrams. The facts don't change. Climate change is natural and cyclical.

The planet has enjoyed cycles of warming and cooling on all different scales and to argue that the current warm period is somehow different from previous warmings is fantasy, not science.

If it is claimed that geology is about the long ago and not about the present, then you would have to show that the fundamental laws of physics and chemistry did not operate in the past and just happen to operate when you are alive. What's happening today is tomorrow's geology.

There are no prizes for guessing what the next cycle will be unless, of course, your presence on planet Earth completely changes major planetary processes. You might be important but not THAT important.

Pleistocene glaciation	110,000 to 14,700 years ago
Bölling	14,700 to 13,900 years ago
Older Dryas	13,900 to 13,600 years ago
Allerød	13,600 to 12,900 years ago
Younger Dryas	12,900 to 11,600 years ago
Holocene warming	11,600 to 8,500 years ago
Egyptian cooling	8,500 to 8,000 years ago
Holocene Warming	8,000 to 5,600 years ago
Akkadian cooling	5,600 to 3,500 years ago
Minoan Warming	3,500 to 3,200 years ago
Bronze Age Cooling	3,200 to 2,500 years ago
Roman Warming	500 BC to 535 AD
Dark Ages	535 AD to 900 AD
Medieval Warming	900 AD to 1300 AD
Little Ice Age	1300 AD to 1850 AD
Modern Warming	1850 AD to ....

Warming and cooling events in the current interglacial derived from sediment, microfossil and chemical information.
Pale =cooling, dark = warming.

We are living on a planet where there has been climate change for 4,567 million years. We are pretty insignificant in the scheme of planetary things and if you think that you can change a major planetary process such as climate change, then you should increase your medication.

If you don't like this planet, move to another one.

WRONG, WRONG and WRONG

The past shows that climate change is unrelated to atmospheric carbon dioxide. The evidence is overwhelming.

We get told over and over and over and over that human emissions drive climate change. The message is shouted so loudly so many times that it's clear the message is propaganda.

Yet we are told that the planet is warming due to human emissions of carbon dioxide and that there will be runaway global warming. Wrong. The planet has cyclical climate changes.

We are told that mythical human-induced global warming will increase the incidence of wildfires, hurricanes, floods and droughts. Wrong. The past shows that these events are unrelated to carbon dioxide. Deaths from climate-related causes have decreased by 98% since the 1920s throughout a period of increasing human emissions of carbon dioxide.

US Forest Area Burned 1926-2017

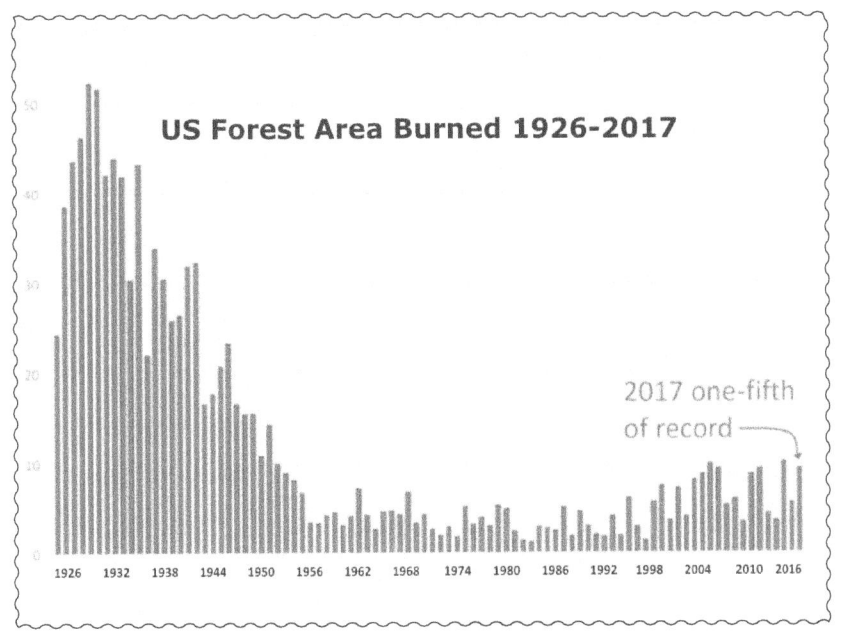

2017 one-fifth of record

Area burnt by US wildfires 1926-2017. If increased atmospheric carbon dioxide created more wildfires, there should have been an increase, not a decrease, in the area burned. The planet is improving, not getting worse.

Ice sheets grow and shrink yet we are told that human emissions of a plant food gas will melt the ice sheets, reduce sea ice and raise sea level. Wrong. The past tells a very different story.

We are told that human emissions of carbon dioxide will warm the planet such that there will be extinctions of species, reefs will disappear and humanity will be threatened. Wrong. The past shows the opposite.

When someone gives you a bad news story time and time

again about the planet, assume it's wrong and that you are being fed disinformation.

If in doubt, follow the money.

A PLANET IN CRISIS

Why do we believe?

Whenever I talk about the planet's past in public, climate zealots attack the man but present no contrary science. We now live in a post-fact time when evidence, knowledge and logic are dismissed.

So why does the idea that human emissions drive climate change continue to dominate popular thinking?

Very few people are employed in the productive segment of the economy. Most are in service, government and administrative roles. The productive segment of the economy does not create climate policy yet suffers from that policy. For example, while the number of people in agriculture has decreased, there has been a 20-fold increase in government bureaucrats over-regulating agriculture. The supply of the food we eat is threatened by stupidity.

Very few people know anything about geology or have been exposed to geology. Almost no schools teach anything about the long history of the planet and most geology departments in universities have been given the kiss of death, closed or amalgamated with environmental science and now present watered-down courses.

Geologists are a rare breed, especially those who have been through a previous rigorous education system. How many geologists do you see or hear interviewed in the media compared to environmentalists, climate activists, green opportunistic politicians and climate "scientists"?

When the idea that human emissions of carbon dioxide drive climate change first appeared, it was the geologists who rolled their eyes. You can count on a sawmiller's hand the number of geologists who think human emissions of carbon dioxide drive climate change. They are those well away from the coal face in politicised taxpayer-funded bureaucracies.

Society has become urbanised with much employment in shiny bum office jobs. Most people now live in cities, very few people want adventures outdoors in the bush all over the world. This requires them to move away from their families and school and university friends for extended periods.

Show me a geologist who has had a boring life. There is travel, risk, excitement, failure and success. Geologists are somewhere out there using deep time to find the commodities you will use in the future. They don't live or work near the centre of media activity.

If they did, it would not make much difference anyway because there is no sensation, disaster or shock-horror story that can be created each day by the mainstream media from good news geology stories.

The media are not about facts, they need to sell and the best way to do this is to frighten the pants off people. Doesn't matter if the story isn't true. By the time their story is shown to be wrong, they have moved onto the next sensational story. The media has a lot to answer for.

Western countries are wealthy compared to the rest of the world. This has been more than a thousand years in the making. The Dutch tulip craze (1634-1637 AD) was when greedy people spent the equivalent of two years pay to buy a rare tulip bulb. When the price of bulbs fell through the floor, a mountain of money was lost and Holland went from being the richest country in the world to a poor country.

Like the Dutch tulip craze, there is excess wealth today which is spent on fads and fashions. Some have an air of unbalanced hysteria. We are now so comfortable because there is nothing to fear. There is no horrible beast lurking behind us looking for its next meal yet evolution has hard wired us to have constant fear. This is exploited by those who benefit from scaring us. We are so wealthy and can afford to waste more than a trillion dollars a year worldwide on renewable energy.

Because so few people have a basic knowledge of science, they can be whipped into fear of the unseen such as radiation, bacteria, viruses and that invisible tasteless odourless gas of life, carbon dioxide.

We are easy prey, especially if we are products of a dumbed down education system where we know little and haven't been taught to think or argue critically. The dumbing down of the education system started in the 1968 student revolutions.

This is exacerbated by social media which requires instant opinions rather than informed opinions based on knowledge, experience, reading and contemplative critical thought.

Contrary to popular belief, the internet is a hive of false information. Even Wikipedia gets my birthdate and career wrong! Disinformation rules. The internet has exploited fear, produced depression and bad decisions and this will get worse with AI.

Western countries are abandoning Christianity, but the concepts of sin, repentance and absolution linger. Environmentalism is the new religion. We are meant to feel guilty by being humans on our own planet. This is a kind of original sin.

Much of the environmental movement is keen on depopulation. I'm happy with this as long as the proponents go first. I promise to follow.

Because we are using the planet for survival, as all other organisms do, we need to pay indulgences which are in the form of carbon taxes and expensive electricity. The faceless unelected leaders of the new religion offer us salvation. Once we have paid up and impoverished ourselves, we may gain absolution.

Those with little to do in their lives and have even less knowledge, join very noisy pressure groups. They are a minority. The majority comprises the average person who works, feeds their family and struggles to give their kids a better life.

They don't have the time, energy or money to be involved in green activism. They are the silent majority who just want to be left in peace and don't want to be told how to think. They can do that for themselves.

Politicians respond to pressure and try to buy votes by pretending to be green. They bend with the wind and most are not concerned about you, your country or your future. They are opportunistic and only want to get re-elected.

Most have law degrees, spent their early years in a party or union office and most have no real-world experience with running a business, farm, factory or mine with all the associated risk, financial stress, long hours and uncertainty.

There are, of course, the rare exceptions. Those who have owned and run businesses or represent rural electorates have a far better understanding of the science of climate than those from city electorates. Every now and then a scientist or engineer becomes a politician. I can think of a couple in Western countries and one Chinese premier (who trained as a geologist).

Politicians have little knowledge of science which makes them easy to bamboozle with catastrophist theories about human emissions of carbon dioxide. If a politician or anyone else does not understand the science, then just follow the money. This will show what climate change is really about.

The past has been ignored. This was easy after 50 years of dumbing down the education system. Climate hysteria and eco-anxiety were promoted by disinformation and all perspective was lost.

What is not considered is that we currently live in the best of times. Ever.

The best of times

The world gross product of the last 2,000 years was static until the late 19th Century and then it rose 1,000-fold concurrent with a decrease in the proportion of the global population in desperate poverty despite the increase in the global population. This was because of coal and oil. Food supply has increased as has the area of forests.

The number of democracies; global happiness; school enrolment worldwide; average years of education; women in politics; global literacy rates; global life expectancy and quality of life; growth of protected areas worldwide; global cereal production and yields; global meat, fish and dairy consumption; global intake of calories; global access to electricity; global access to improved potable water and sanitation; global access to mobile phones; oil and gas reserves have risen contrary to peak oil hysteria; and the internet and global international tourism all have increased. Since the time of Jesus, global GDP *per capita* has increased 30,000 times.

Autocracies, wars, deaths from natural disasters, global death rate, infant mortality, maternal mortality, global homicide and battle deaths, military expenditure and nuclear warheads, births per woman, people living in slums, average hours worked in high income countries, work-related deaths, wage gap in high income countries, the number of countries with legal slavery and child labour, global income inequality, carbon dioxide emissions per dollar of GDP, global undernourishment rate, global hours worked to produce one unit of a commodity and average cost of computer storage all have decreased.

Over the last 50 years in the lifetime of your grandparents, global *per capita* GDP, longevity, health, crop land productivity and forests have increased due to technology, use of fossil fuels and a slight increase in plant food in the air.

We are now feeding more people from less land. Global pollution has decreased. The planet is improving after a bit of a bashing by previous generations.

Green activists ignore the fact that we live in the best time ever to be a human on planet Earth. Rather than trying to bring us back to the horrible times centuries ago, they should be positive and try to make the world an even better place. If you think things are bad today, get into managing the country and making it better than it is now.

If green activists disagree, they should give up everything that the last five generations using cheap fossil fuel brought them. Go and live in a cave as a hunter-gatherer, travel using a unicorn dust-powered machine and see how you survive.

If green activists or school children on strike are to be taken seriously, they should demonstrate in Tiananmen Square against the world's biggest emitter of carbon dioxide and should give up the use of all electronic equipment.

Cheap energy

Wealth and abundant cheap reliable energy have solved environmental problems, not green activists. As a result, food has become more abundant, healthier and cheaper.

Fossil fuel energy has led to a great increase in health, diet, longevity, wealth and leisure over the last five generations of humans using any measure we choose. There was no change in people's lives over the previous 20,000 generations of humans. Change was brought about by fossil fuels.

Coal brought people out of grinding poverty and misery in the Northern Hemisphere Industrial Revolution and later hundreds of millions of Chinese out of crippling poverty. Green activists want to ban the use of fossil fuels in an attempt to reverse these gains.

When green activists, politicians and celebrities live in caves as sustainable hunter gatherers, we may seek their advice. While they travel around the world in private jets to chastise us for our emissions of carbon dioxide, they are lying hypocrites.

After thousands of years of poverty, the developing world, especially Asia, is using more and more coal to generate electricity. You now have a healthy, long life due to coal. By denying people coal, the end result will be killing people.

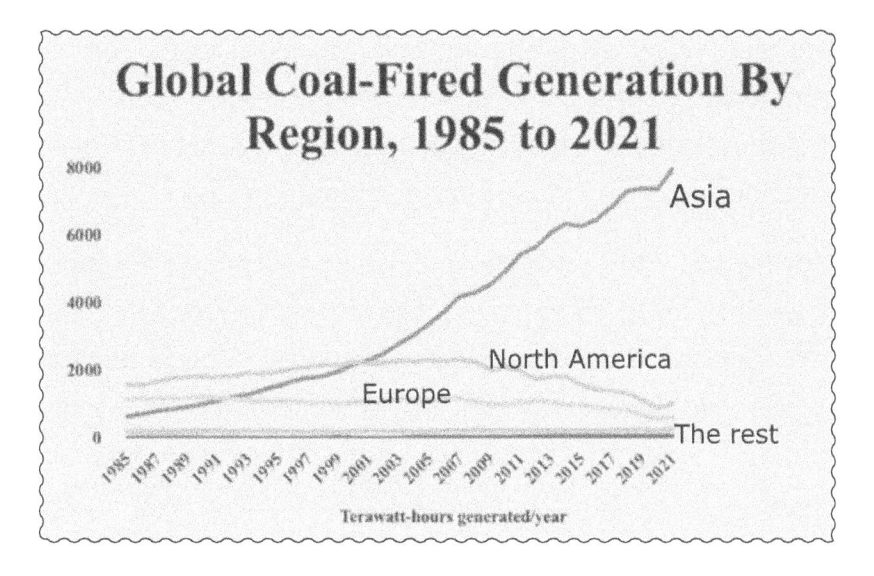

Global Coal-Fired Generation By Region, 1985 to 2021

Electricity generation by coal over the last five decades.

Communist China is building six times as much coal-fired power as the rest of the world. Capitalist Australia exports almost 400 million tonnes of coal each year for other countries to burn in power stations for electricity and to make steel.

Simultaneously, there is pressure in Australia to stop using coal to produce reliable coal-fired electricity locally. Whatever Australia does makes no difference to the planet as it accounts for about 1% of annual human emissions of carbon dioxide.

The world has changed from a rural subsistence population in brutal poverty to a city-based population employed in service industries. Because of geology, mines are in isolated areas and food growing is outside cities in rural areas. Both are mechanised requiring far fewer people than the service sector. City people are detached from the processes involved to bring them their food, fibre, fuel, fish and metals. Cheap reliable energy is required for everything we use.

For the last 120 years, fossil fuels have accounted for more than 80% of all energy used. Energy use is increasing and wind and solar have not made a dent. The biggest electric power stations in the world are now hydro and nuclear. In some countries of low rainfall and a flattened topography, hydro is not suitable. Fossil fuels produce over 6,000 commodities used in everyday life.

Burning more fossil fuels per person means less polluted air if you live in a wealthy democratic Western country. The biggest energy users are also the cleanest countries. This is a good news story you will never hear in the mainstream media. Why? Because it is good news and not some shock horror disaster.

There are over 2,400 operating coal-fired power stations in the world. Civilisation has advanced one coal-fired power station at a time. Closing English, European, Canadian or Australian coal-fired power stations will have no effect whatsoever on global carbon dioxide emissions.

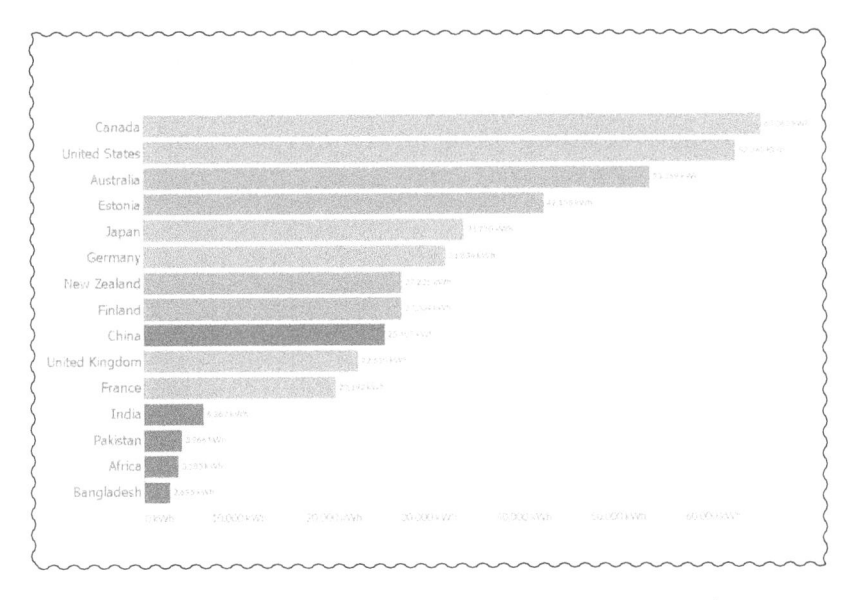

Fossil fuel consumption showing that the cleanest countries are the biggest consumers of fossil fuels.

Australia has 24 operating coal-fired power stations compared to the operating plants in China (1,118), the European Union (256), USA (224) and India (179). There are 9 operating coal-fired power stations in Canada and 2 in the UK.

The massive 2.6 GW Drax power station is in the UK. European Union regulations state that wood is renewable energy. This resulted in Drax changing from coal to using wood harvested from virgin forests in the US. Wood is pelletised using fossil fuel energy and transported by fossil fuel-burning ships across the Atlantic Ocean.

Burning wood emits carbon dioxide into the atmosphere. The UK is cheating on its carbon dioxide emissions using European Union false accounting. Is this really environmentalism?

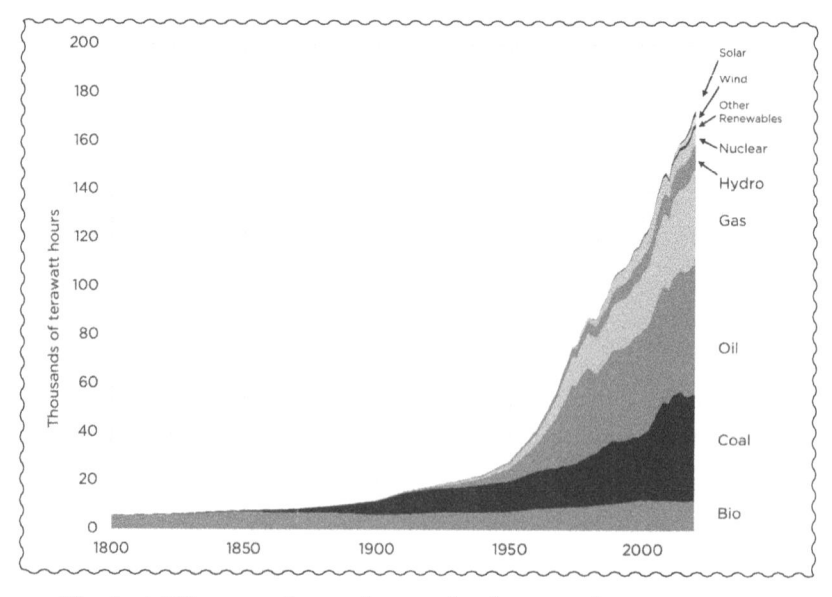

The last 200 years shows the massive increase in energy use as people escaped serfdom into the modern industrial world. Wind and solar have contributed next to nothing to the global energy use.

The political solution to speculated future catastrophic climate change driven by emissions of carbon dioxide was to demonise carbon dioxide and to try to reduce human emissions of carbon dioxide. This attracted votes. Coal-fired power stations which provided 24/7 electricity were closed to reduce carbon dioxide emissions.

Sea breezes and sunbeams

Governments panicked and tried to solve a non-problem with inefficient technology that spears the countryside and seas with wind turbines and covers prime farming land with solar panels. Wind generates electricity for 24 minutes an hour. Which 24 minutes is anybody's guess. This is the problem with wind. No economy can have such uncertainty.

To make investment possible in inefficient electricity generation systems, governments have provided huge incentives, subsidies and a controlled expensive electricity market.

The only thing renewable about renewable energy are the subsidies. They just keep coming and coming and are hidden in a dodgy highly complex electricity pricing structure and taxes.

The energy used to build a wind or solar facility is far greater than the energy they will ever produce. The carbon dioxide emissions from manufacturing wind and solar facilities are far more than emissions saved by closing coal-fired power stations.

Wind turbine blades slice and dice bats and birds and create health problems for those living nearby. Offshore wind turbines are far bigger and kill whales and drop oil into the oceans.

Wind turbines destroy scenic views, are a navigation hazard and pristine rainforest inland from the Great Barrier Reef has been flattened to build a wind complex. Is this environmentalism?

Turbine blades comprise layers of balsa wood and epoxy resin. To make blades, Amazon rainforest balsa trees need to be cut down and highly toxic chemicals in epoxy resins such as bisphenol-A are used in the blades.

Bisphenol-A is banned in many countries. The blades erode and spread bisphenol-A far and wide into soils and the waterways and the blades cannot be recycled after their short life. They are cut up, dumped and bisphenol-A leaks into soils and waterways. Is this what you want? Emissions of the plant food carbon dioxide are far better for the planet.

The rare earth elements in wind turbines are mined in China, the radioactive uranium- and thorium-rich wastes are dumped and spread over a wide area of land. Most turbine blades are manufactured in China.

If you are a supporter of wind power for environmental reasons, you are also responsible for radioactive contamination of large areas of the planet.

It is not possible to be an environmentalist and support the generation of electricity from wind turbines, unless of course you are a hypocrite or are making money from subsidies to the wind business.

It will be your generation that is responsible for cleaning up the mess made by your parent's generation in the name of environmentalism. This is a case of having to destroy the environment to save the planet.

Slave labour in China makes the silicon solar panels. Lead, cadmium, selenium and tellurium in solar panels are highly toxic and are spread over huge areas during rain. Prime agricultural land for production of food is covered with thousands of hectares of solar panels. This is not environmentalism.

When the Sun's rays hit solar panels, electricity and heat are generated. In many places during summer, the panels overheat and can't be used. Electricity from coal-fired generators must then be used for air conditioning, fans, refrigerators, cooking and just keeping the lights on.

Those supporting solar electricity claim that solar energy will reduce global warming. If the panels must be shut down in summer, then they are useless in preventing global warming.

The Sun does not shine all the time and the wind does not constantly blow. There are long periods of time when there is no wind, called wind droughts. This has been known by sailors for thousands of years. During a wind drought, the wind companies still get paid despite not generating electricity. Energy prices go through the roof and you pay. Wind droughts can last more than a week.

Solar and wind energy do not provide the 24/7 electricity generated from coal, nuclear, gas or hydro. They are not free. There needs to be expensive back up for solar and wind. Battery back-up is prohibitively expensive and only provides power, at most, for an hour or so. No city has ever survived on batteries.

To build a 100 MW gas turbine, 300 tonnes of iron ore, 2,000 tonnes of concrete and 100 tonnes of special metals are used on an area the size of a household block.

To build a 100 MW wind turbine complex, 30,000 tonnes of iron ore, 30,000 tonnes of concrete, 1,000 tonnes of special metals and 800 tonnes of plastics are used in an area of 26 square kilometres of land.

Which technology is better for the environment?

Fads, fashions, fools and fires

You do not reduce emissions or save the planet by driving an electric vehicle (EV). It's the exact opposite. Driving an EV solves nothing, creates unforeseen problems, costs a fortune and is highly inefficient. At least 80,000 km need to be driven to pay back the amount of carbon dioxide emitted during EV manufacture.

EVs use six times as much metal as conventional cars. Going green by using an EV requires far more and far larger mines than exist at present. A huge amount of copper is used in EVs. For every tonne of copper used in an EV, at least 200 tonnes of copper ore must be dug up, about the same tonnage of tailings need to be stored and hundreds of tonnes of waste rock is moved and dumped. All this is done using diesel-driven machines.

We have not yet discovered the copper deposits needed to produce the copper required for EVs. These will be found mainly in Third World countries. The great rich copper deposits were found at surface. They are now finished or currently being mined.

We are now mining rocks with less and less copper and at greater depths. This produces even larger waste dumps and tailings dams with minerals that react with water and air to produce acid drainage.

If the world's 1.5 billion vehicles are swapped for EVs, we would need 944 million tonnes of lithium. Around 26 million tonnes of lithium reserves are currently defined on the planet. What happens if someone invents a better battery than the lithium battery?

Lithium batteries in EVs use cobalt mined by black slave children in the Congo. Many die in dangerous deep open cuts and underground mines. Others are poisoned by cobalt. China controls cobalt mining in the Congo. For every tonne of cobalt metal used in an EV, around 1,500 tonnes of cobalt ore needs to be mined.

EV drivers must be huge supporters of the mining industry and child slavery and are responsible for the environmental mess in poor Third World countries. Feel good?

When you swan around in your EV feeling morally superior to those in their efficient fossil fuel vehicles, do you ever spare a thought for the child slaves that died to provide metal for your EV?

China controls the basic commodities used in EVs such as lithium, cobalt, nickel and graphite. It is now the biggest car manufacturer in the world.

In the UK, drivers are buying petrol and diesel vehicles rather than EVs. There is a lack of charging stations, massive loss of value after purchase of a very high-cost vehicle, eye-wateringly high repair costs and difficulties in travel, even for small distances and especially in winter.

Safety features such as being unable to get out of the car when it runs out of charge and battery fires make EVs unattractive. Governments are trying to force people to drive inefficient EVs without investing the trillions of dollars necessary to change the whole electricity grid. That's money that could go to housing and health.

EV insurers are reluctant to attempt repairs for even the most minor battery damage which can be caused by something as small as mounting the kerb or getting a dent from a rock. EVs are written off because there are so few technicians qualified to safely repair EVs. Is this environmentalism?

Some ferry owners refuse to carry EVs and some car parks don't allow EVs because of the fire risk. Many EVs cannot be charged in apartment blocks because of circuit overload.

EVs don't go far, the battery degrades quickly, a huge amount of time is wasted with charging, there are few charging stations, they cost a fortune, maintenance and insurance is crippling, they are worth next to nothing after a few years use, they catch alight and whole new electricity grids need to be built to charge them.

If you cared for the environment and your fellow humans, you would not use cobalt and would not drive an EV that was destined for landfill after a short life.

Compared to all other energy sources, hydrogen is the most efficient fuel but it comes with insurmountable problems. So do lithium batteries, the most inefficient energy source.

Fuel	Value
Lithium Battery	0.5
Wood	17.1
Ethanol	19.9
Coal (Bituminous)	23.9
Methanol	31.1
Coal (Anthracite)	31.4
Bunker C	40.0
Crude Oil	41.9
Jet A-1	43.3
Diesel	45.3
Gasoline (Automobile)	45.8
Kerosene	46.3
Natural Gas	47.2
Propane	50.3
LNG	55.0
Methane	55.5
Hydrogen	142.0

Energy efficiency of natural and manufactured fuels.

Hydrogen was tried as a fuel in the 19th and 20th Centuries and failed. Hydrogen must be manufactured and cannot be mined. Because it is too expensive to make and uses more energy to make than it will ever produce, the numbers just don't add up. Hydrogen must be stored as liquid hydrogen at 700 times atmospheric pressure and at minus 253°C.

A huge amount of energy is needed to create these conditions. Hydrogen is such a small molecule that it diffuses through solid steel, especially at high pressure, and stored hydrogen leaks out very quickly. As soon as hydrogen diffuses through steel, the steel is greatly weakened.

Hydrogen is super explosive. If you want to take a risk with a catastrophic explosion, play with hydrogen. We've only known this since 1766 AD. Hydrogen is the new laughing gas.

Change your life

You are being told by activists to:

Reduce emissions of carbon dioxide, plant food, by 80% by 2030 yet those who are telling you this are not doing it themselves.

Reduce emissions to an undefined Net Zero by 2050.

Completely rebuild the whole electricity infrastructure with a duplicated system at an unaffordable cost by 2030.

Pay increased costs for electricity and everything else.

Go down the energy path of Germany and the UK, both of whom have suffered massive hardship, cost of living increase, loss of industry, loss of jobs just to try to feel good about reducing emissions and achieving nothing.

Reduce emissions that will bring you to poverty levels while the biggest emitters (China, India, USA) merrily increase their emissions.

Cut back on your own electricity and fossil fuel use, travel less and change your diet while your political masters and their bureaucrats remain connected to the grid, travel whenever and wherever they want in cars, planes and ships and eat speciality foods, all at your expense.

The evidence I present gives the opposite story to what you have heard in schools, universities and the mainstream media.

The planet is certainly in a crisis. There is just not enough carbon dioxide in the atmosphere for long-term plant survival yet we live in the best times ever to be a human on the planet.

Our wealth, dumbed down education system and the internet has produced Peter Pans with a desperate desire not to face the realities of the adult world and a hunger for attention, not from their own achievements, but by exhibitionist antics.

Get a life. Be different, think independently.

For twenties and wrinklies

Ian Plimer's Books

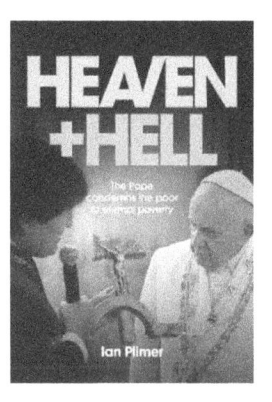

how to get expelled from school
A guide to climate change for pupils, parents & punters
Ian Plimer

GREEN MURDER
A LIFE SENTENCE OF NET ZERO WITH NO PAROLE
IAN PLIMER

not for greens
Ian Plimer

Climate change delusion and the great electricity rip-off
Ian Plimer

HEAVEN + HELL
The Pope condemns the poor to eternal poverty
Ian Plimer

heaven+earth
Global Warming: The Missing Science
Ian Plimer

connorcourt

Scan code

Sources

Alley, N. 2000: The Younger Dryas cold interval as viewed from central Greenland. *Journal of Quaternary Science Reviews* 19, 213-226

Berner, R. A. and Kothavala, Z., 2001: GEOCARB III: A revised model of atmospheric CO_2 over Phanerozoic time. *American Journal of Science* 301, 182-204

Dudok de Wit, T., Kopp, G., Fröhlich, C. and Schöll, M., 2017: Methodology to create a new Total Solar Irradiance record: Making a composite out of total data records. *Geophysical Research Letters* doi: 10.1002/2016GL071866

https://www.clintel.org An international European-based foundation for climate change and climate policy comprising scientists.

https://www.co2coalition.org The coalition is a non-partisan educational foundation addressing the policy issues of carbon dioxide, climate and science. It is one of the most informative WWW sites on the role of carbon dioxide and climate change. They publish unchallengeable climate facts.

https://www.electroverse.co An outstanding site with a focus on earth changes during the grand solar minimum and space weather with a focus on anomalous cold weather in times of global "boiling".

https://www.ipa.org.au An Australian free market institute that has been a force in politics since 1943. The author is a member and benefactor of the IPA.

http://www.joannenova.com.au One of the most popular and best climate sites in the world. Jo Nova uses logic, science and humour to discuss the latest claims by climate activists, hypocrites and frauds. Essential daily reading.

http://www.geocraft.com A great general site on geology, the history of the planet, evolution and climate over time.

https://geology.utah.gov/map-pub/survey-notes/glad-you-asked/ice-ages-what-are-they-and-what-causes-them/ This is one of many geological sites that looks back in time at climate change. All have a similar reconstruction of past temperatures and carbon dioxide over time based on ice core drilling, sediment and fossil analysis and proxies.

https://jennifermarahasy.com The site of an Australian biologist who researches the measurement techniques of Australia's Bureau of Meteorology, the Great Barrier Reef and climate. Source of data, films, scientific publications and scientific expertise contrary to that presented by the mainstream media.

https://www.heartland.org A conservative political site that inter alia deals with climate.

https://www.iea.org The International Energy Agency is an invaluable site for coal, oil, nuclear, energy generation and reserves.

Loehle, C. 2007: A 2000-year global temperature reconstruction based on non-tree ring proxies. *Energy and Environment* 18, 1049-1058

https://www.ncel.NOAA.gov is another source of primary data through NOAA, NASA and the National Centers for Environmental Information. One needs patience to trawl through this site which displays, for example, the global warming in the scale of human temperature experience compared to the magnified warming as presented by the media. The National Temperature Index can be used to use time series temperature in the US. This is an absolute essential site for understanding climate.

https://www.msstc.uah.edu The Alabama Office of the State Climatologist, John R Christy of the University of Alabama at Huntsville (https://www.uah.edu) documents the earth's temperature from satellites, measures extreme weather events and compares models with data from balloons and satellites. Christy gives the most reliable uncontaminated data on global temperature.

Petit, J. R., Jouzel, J., Raynaud, D., Barkov, N. I., Barnola, J.-M., Basile, I., Bender, M., Chappellaz, J., Davis, M., Derlaygue, G., Delmotte, M., Kotlyakov, V. M., Legrand, M., Lipenjkov, V. Y., Lorius, C., Pépin, Ritz, C., Saltzman, E. and Stievenard, M., 1999: Climate and atmospheric history of the past 420,000 years from the Vostok ice core, Antarctica. *Nature* 399, 429-426

Petkova, E. P., Gasparrini, A. and Kinney, P. L. 2014: Heat and mortality in New York City since the beginning of the 20th Century. *Epidemiology* 25(4), 554-560

https://www.prageru.com is a site that finds primary data hidden on official sites and then questions the popular scary narrative presented by the mainstream media and those with a self-interest.

https://public.wmo.int The World Meteorological Organization which is a source of primary data on world death rate from hurricanes, storms and climate, weather-related disasters, global burned areas etc.

Scotese, C. R. 2002: *Analysis of the temperature oscillations in geological eras*. W. H Freeman and Co., New York

http://www.thegwpf.org A UK-based foundation that deals with the politics and policy of global warming, mainly in the UK but globally. The author sits on the Global Warming Policy Foundation Scientific Advisory Board.

https://www.thrivingwithfire.org A US site showing how fires, a natural restorative force, are driven by weather, arson, fuel load etc and not climate.

https://www.wattsupwiththat.com is a very popular site of meteorologist Anthony Watts that deals with weather, climate, the latest media exaggerations and analyses official government data. For example, the NOAA average temperature anomaly of the US Climate Reference Network is updated every few weeks, the main stream media never search for the detailed data and sites like WUWT find and publish the data that is contrary to the narrative.

Wu, C.-J., Krivova, N. A., Solanki, S. K. and Ulsoskin, I. G. 2018: Solar total and spectral irradiance reconstruction over the last 9000 years. *Astronomy and Astrophysics* 620, doi.org/10.1051/0004-6361/201832956

Zharkova, V. 2020: Modern Grand Solar Minimum will lead to terrestrial cooling. Temperature 7, 217-222

Scientific, philosophical and psychological writings by John Christy, Judith Curry, Alex Epstein, Willis Eschenbach, Will Happer, Steven Koonin, Mark Lawson, Nigel Lawson, Richard Lindzen, Christopher Monckton, Patrick Moore, Andrew Montford, Jordan Peterson, Nir Shaviv, Michael Shellenberger, Henrik Svensmark and Valentina Zharkova form the basis of background reading for this book. Activist and blatantly disinformative sites such as Wikipedia, Skeptical science and DeSmog Blog were also visited to keep abreast of the latest scams.